*The Observer's Pocket Series*
SEA AND SEASHORE

# The Observer Books

A POCKET REFERENCE SERIES COVERING A
WIDE RANGE OF SUBJECTS

---

## Natural History

BIRDS
BIRD'S EGGS
BUTTERFLIES
LARGER MOTHS
COMMON INSECTS
WILD ANIMALS
ZOO ANIMALS
WILD FLOWERS
GARDEN FLOWERS
FLOWERING TREES
          AND SHRUBS
HOUSE PLANTS
CACTI
TREES
GRASSES
FERNS
COMMON FUNGI
LICHENS
POND LIFE
FRESHWATER FISHES
SEA FISHES
SEA AND SEASHORE
GEOLOGY
ASTRONOMY
WEATHER
CATS
DOGS
HORSES AND PONIES

## Transport

AIRCRAFT
AUTOMOBILES
COMMERCIAL VEHICLES
SHIPS
MANNED SPACEFLIGHT

## The Arts etc

ARCHITECTURE
CATHEDRALS
CHURCHES
HERALDRY
FLAGS
PAINTING
MODERN ART
SCULPTURE
FURNITURE
MUSIC
POSTAGE STAMPS

## Sport

ASSOCIATION FOOTBALL
CRICKET

## Cities

LONDON

# The Observer's Book of
# SEA AND SEASHORE

Edited by
I. O. EVANS, F.R.G.S.

*ALL ASPECTS DESCRIBED*
*with 64 plates in colour and*
*monochrome, 48 of which are*
*by Ernest C. Mansell*

FREDERICK WARNE & CO LTD
FREDERICK WARNE & CO INC
LONDON · NEW YORK

© FREDERICK WARNE & CO. LTD.
LONDON, ENGLAND
1962
*Sixth reprint* 1973


LIBRARY OF CONGRESS CATALOG CARD
NUMBER 62-12501


ISBN   0   7232   0073   4


*Printed in Great Britain*

1272.573

# CONTENTS

# LIST OF PLATES

# INTRODUCTION

*' They that go down to the sea in ships and do their
business in great waters: these see the works of the
Lord and His wonders in the deep.'*

These words are as true today as when they were
first spoken, nor do they apply only to those whose
business takes them down to the sea in ships.
They that go down to the sea simply for recreation
and enjoyment and are content to remain on the
edge of the great waters will nevertheless see many
works and wonders in the deep. The aim of the
author in writing this book is to avoid burdening
the observer with overmuch detail or needless
technical terms but to increase his appreciation of
the outdoor world by summarizing some of the
findings of the relevant branches of natural history.

There are already many excellent books on the
animals and plants which live on the coast or in
the offshore waters. Non-technical descriptions of
the coast itself and of the sea which washes it are
harder to come by. This book seeks to cover both
these aspects, the sea and the seashore as well as
the living creatures which inhabit them.

A brief description of the sea is followed by an
account of its movements, the waves which con-
vulse its surface and the tides and currents which
send it swirling round the coast. This leads
naturally to a discussion of its action on the land,
the forces which carve the rocks into jagged cliffs
and smooth the sands of the beach. Then is
summarized the evidence for the mighty earth
movements which have submerged long stretches

9

of the coastline and raised vast areas of the sea-floor to form dry land.

There follows what many observers may find the most interesting part of the subject, the living creatures of the shore and the sea. Not only are the most common of these described, but something is also said about their strange ways of life and the even more surprising changes which some of them undergo before they reach maturity. The book also glances at the natural ' communities ' which inhabit regions as diverse, for example, as the damp sands of the beaches and the pools among the sunbaked rocks.

The scientific terms are given partly because, being international, they may prove helpful to visitors from overseas, and partly because they facilitate deeper study of the fascinating subject of marine biology. Technical terms are otherwise avoided as much as possible, though some are essential, the creatures which bear them having no commonplace names.

The second part of the book, on the living creatures of the sea and seashore, is based on information supplied by Dr. J. C. Smyth, to whom I am greatly indebted. I am also grateful to Mr. W. G. Teagle for many helpful suggestions in connection with the material on sea-birds and mammals.

During the many visits which I have been able to make to the seashore, I have found my pleasure greatly enhanced by my interest in the subjects which this book discusses. If I can impart that increased pleasure and interest to the reader, I shall be glad indeed.

I. O. E.

# THE SEA

## CHARACTER AND COMPOSITION

The *sea*, or *ocean*, is a vast expanse of salt water, covering about seven-tenths of the earth, and filling almost all its depressions. Its surface area is about 140,000,000 square miles; its depth, about 30,000 feet at greatest, averages some 13,000 feet. Echo-soundings have shown that the sea-floor, or ocean-bed, is extremely irregular, being traversed by countless rises and grooves and broken by *deeps* like submarine canyons, *ridges* like submerged mountain ranges, steep-sided *earth-pillars* whose tips form the oceanic islands, and *sea-mounts* of volcanic origin.

Round the great land masses the sea-floor slopes gently down from the shore to a depth of several hundred feet; round the British Isles and off Newfoundland this *continental shelf* is hundreds of miles wide, but in some places it is quite narrow. Beyond the shelf the *continental slope* dips more sharply to several thousand feet, and from its foot extends the *abyss*. Shelf and slope are traversed by many deep grooves, some prolonging the river valleys of the land, others having no relation to them.

Apart from its ripples and waves, the surface of the ocean seems level, but this apparent flatness is of course an illusion. The masts and sails, or the funnel smoke, of a ship may be visible though her hull is hidden below the horizon, and her own crow's nest brings into sight objects invisible from her deck.

This affords evidence of the earth's shape, the whole surface of land and sea being a sphere somewhat flattened at the poles; hence the impossibility of mapping large areas correctly on a flat surface. Circumnavigation of the earth in various directions further demonstrates its shape; and, seen or photographed from far aloft, its 'edge' appears not as a straight line but as a curve.

## CHEMICAL COMPOSITION

The 'salt sea' is not merely salty but bitter. It consists of *brine*, a strong solution of material washed down from the land; sodium chloride (common salt) predominates, but many other chemicals are present, with traces at least of all the elements. The strength of the solution averages about 3·5 per cent, being weaker round the ice-fields, somewhat stronger in the land-locked Mediterranean and Red seas, and far stronger in such inland waters as the Dead Sea.

The sea also holds in suspension much sand and silt, countless living creatures and the waste products and dead bodies of others, along with such materials as sewage, factory effluents, detergents, crude oil and radio-active waste. Small wonder, then, that to drink sea water only increases thirst and may lead to madness and death! Recently, however, claims have been made that when mixed with the body fluids of fish brine will sustain life, so long as the constitution is not already weakened by prolonged thirst.

When sea water freezes, or when it evaporates or boils, its salts crystallize out, only the water itself becoming ice or steam. Fresh water may be obtained by melting ice or distilling brine (boiling it and condensing the steam), and salt is won from the sea by letting brine evaporate either, as on the coast of Brittany, in artificial salt-pans or, as on that of Australia, in shallow depressions in the rocks.

## EVAPORATION

Whenever water is exposed to the air it evaporates, its surface layers rising into the air as an invisible vapour; the immense volumes evaporated from the sea accumulate as clouds. The warmer and drier the air, and the more intense the sunshine, the greater is the evaporation.

The material washed down from the land by the rivers does not evaporate. Hence the sea is growing increasingly salty, though some of the material is deposited on the shore and some goes to build the bodies of its inhabitants. The change is very gradual and will take millions of years to become noticeable; it is more rapid in enclosed waters than in the open sea, making the Mediterranean more salty than the North Atlantic near by.

## THE 'FEEL' OF SEA WATER

This dissolved material makes the brine feel a little slimy ; though it stings unpleasantly on cuts and grazes, it also acts as a mild disinfectant. Anything wetted with sea water always remains slightly damp, as the salts deposited when it evaporates are hygroscopic, attracting moisture from the air. Ordinary soap, being meant for use only in fresh water, will not lather in brine, special brands being needed.

## BUOYANCY

The material it holds in solution makes the specific gravity of brine greater than that of pure water, so the light objects float more buoyantly on the sea than on inland waters, and heavier objects are easier to support or lift. The *Plimsoll marks* on the sides of ships indicate the loads they can safely carry under different conditions, and of these *load lines* that applicable to fresh water is highest. Its greater buoyancy similarly makes swimming or floating easier in the sea than in inland waters.

## THE COLOUR OF THE SEA

The colour of the sea is modified by the particles which float in it ; by the angle from which it is viewed ; by the clearness of the day ; by reflection from the sky, the clouds or the adjacent cliffs; and, in the shallows, by the colour of the sea-floor. It varies from a dull leaden grey in gloomy weather, or from the yellow or brown of a muddy river mouth, to a delightful blue or green; off parts of the coast of Cornwall it is given a milky appearance by effluent from the China clay workings. Seen on a bright summer's day from the cliff tops it may be a rich purple—the 'wine-coloured sea' of the Greek classical poets.

Light shining through a wave crest gives a momentary glimpse of translucent green, best observed from the interior of a sea-cave. The billows that break on a coral-reef are many-coloured by reflection from the coral animals that live on the face of the reef.

Water has a slightly bluish tint, and this intercepts the reds and yellows of the daylight much more quickly than the other colours, so that only the blues and greens can penetrate to any depth below the surface; a white object sinking into the water turns blue before passing out of sight. Beneath the sea objects appear in their usual colours only when they are floodlit by a strong white light and viewed from a short distance; when either the observer or the light moves away from them they appear increasingly blue.

Finely divided drops of water always look intensely white, so that the spray from a breaking wave is literally whiter than the snow; compared with the spray, indeed, the snow seems almost drab. In the wake left by a moving vessel the white foam contrasts with the colours of the undisturbed water, and still more strikingly with the emerald green or azure blue of the water churned up from below.

## REFLECTION AND REFRACTION

Only when its surface is perfectly calm, in sheltered rock-pools and the like, does the sea give clear *reflections*. These are normally broken by the waves and ripples, often producing a shimmer of light. The glare of sunshine on the sea can be painfully dazzling, but the gentle glow of moonbeams on the waves is beautiful, and the multicoloured shore and harbour lights give picturesque reflections.

*Refraction* is the ' kinking ' of a ray of light which occurs whenever it passes from air into water or from water into air (or into any other liquid). This makes submerged objects seem nearer the surface than they really are, so that what looks like a shallow rock-pool may be disconcertingly deep.

When the eyes are opened under water everything looks blurred, the light being refracted at the curved surface of the eyeball, where the light passes from the water into the fluids within the eye. This effect can be obviated by wearing special goggles which enable the strange underwater scenery and its even stranger inhabitants to be seen more clearly. An aqualung or frogman's skin-diving equipment, and a waterproof camera, enable submarine photographs to be taken.

**Plate I** The rocky coastline at Land's End (p. 55).

B

HEATING AND COOLING

Water has a very high *specific heat* : it warms up, and cools down, more slowly than most other substances. On a mild spring morning the sea may still be unpleasantly chilly ; contrasting with the nipping air of autumn, it may be delightfully warm.

For the same reason the ocean retains warmth —or coldness—and its currents transport this across the world with marked effects on the climate. The coast of north-west Europe is washed by the warm Gulf Stream and that of north-eastern America by a cold current from the Arctic ; hence though the British Isles are in about the same latitude as Labrador, their climate is much more temperate.

CONVECTION CURRENTS

Except when about to freeze, water contracts in cooling, and becomes heavier. In winter the surface layers of the ocean, cooled by the chill air, sink below the warmer water beneath ; some of this rises to take its place, only to be cooled and sink back. This has produced a system of *convection currents* which keep the water in movement and prevent stagnation.

These currents bring to the surface, where plants and animals can use them, such substances essential to life as phosphates and nitrates. Those operating in the far south are especially powerful, and the rich material they carry provides food for countless living creatures, including the Antarctic whales. On the other hand it is a disquieting thought that if radio-active waste were recklessly dumped into the ocean depths, the currents might distribute it widely, with disastrous results.

If water kept on contracting as it froze, ice would be too heavy to float. Sinking to the sea-floor, where it would be out of reach of the summer's warmth, it would accumulate ever more thickly and spread ever more widely, while the rest of the sea would become increasingly saturated with salt. Except for a surface layer of concentrated brine, the whole ocean might become a solid mass of ice.

As, however, the freezing water no longer contracts but expands and gets lighter, the ice floats. Accumulating on the surface, it protects the depths below from the chill air ; and in the summer most of it melts. Thus the ice-fields are restricted to the polar regions, and the great bulk of the sea never freezes at all.

### INERTIA AND FLUIDITY

Like everything else, sea water is inert, and to move it or check or divert its flow requires some form of force. Like all other fluids, however, it yields to a thrust and adapts its flow to obstacles. It resists a sudden blow but is readily cleft by streamlined objects ; to fall flat on its surface is painful, so the diver plunges head foremost and protects his head and shoulders by raising his arms to form a wedge.

This combination of *fluidity* and *inertia* makes swimming and navigation possible. While the limbs of the swimmer thrust the water backward, it resists the thrust sufficiently to propel him forward, and parts before him to let him proceed. The oars of the rower likewise thrust the water backward, but again its resistance drives the oars forward, and these propel the boat, its streamlined prow enabling it to cleave the water. The paddles of a steamer, except that they too thrust the water backwards, act like the driving wheels of a locomotive or car. A ship's propeller screws its way through the water like a huge corkscrew or gimlet, the spiral twist of the blades moving the water in one direction and the vessel in another.

A rudder held amidships keeps a vessel on course. Thrust to port or starboard, at an angle with the ship, it diverts the water obliquely sideways, and the water pressure tends to thrust the rudder in the opposite direction ; the rudder takes the stern of the vessel with it, so making her pivot round her centre of gravity. Then the rudder is again held amidships to keep her on her new course.

Landsmen are often bewildered to know that a sailing-vessel can travel obliquely against an adverse wind ; this is made possible only by the water's resistance.

As it blows against the sail, the wind of course presses against this ; at the same time it reduces the pressure of the air on the opposite side of the sail and, so to speak, ' sucks ' it to leeward. When the

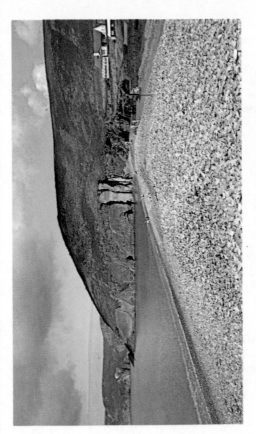

**Plate 2**  Storm beach at Newgale, St. Bride's Bay, Pembrokeshire (p. 66).

wind is perpendicular to the sail, as in a square-rigged ship running before the wind, it drives the vessel forward.

When, however, it blows obliquely against the sail, its thrust acts as though it consisted of two less powerful thrusts, at right angles to one another. One of these thrusts is along the surface of the sail and hardly affects it at all. The other is perpendicular to the sail and tends to drive the ship sideways, but is kept from doing so by the resistance of the water against the vessel's hull and against her keel or centreboard (Fig. 1(a) ).

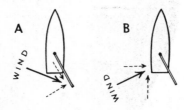

Fig. 1. Tacking motion of a sailing-vessel

This second thrust also acts as if it consisted of two less powerful ones : one, at right angles to the vessel's side, affects her but slightly ; the other, which is along her length, drives her forward, a movement facilitated by her tapering prow (Fig. 1(b) ).

A skilful helmsman, on a well-built vessel, can make her sail surprisingly ' near the wind '. Needless to say she cannot possibly sail directly into it ; to progress against a head wind she has to make a series of *tacks*, swerving now to one side of the wind, now to the other.

# WAVES

## WINDS AND WAVES

The pressure of the wind makes the surface of the sea undulate, alternately rising and falling in a series of waves : ridges of water, the *wave crests*, are separated by *troughs*, the waves being perpendicular to the wind and driven before it. Their *length* is the distance between two successive crests ; their *height* is the vertical distance from the top of the crest to the bottom of the trough ; their *speed* is the rate at which they pass any motionless object ; and their *period* is the time which two successive wave crests take to pass it.

The greater the length of the waves, the faster they travel. The small waves, the *ripples*, move slowly ; but it is not only the height and steepness of the great Atlantic combers but also their speed which makes them dangerous. The danger is increased by the small steep-faced waves which form on the gentler slopes of the large billows.

The stronger the wind, the higher the waves ; their violence is also increased by their *fetch*, the distance they are blown across the sea. In sheltered waters even a strong wind has too small a fetch to produce large waves ; it simply makes the sea choppy. In the open, where the fetch is great, the waves grow higher and longer and travel faster.

In the Atlantic, where the gales, though strong, have a limited fetch, the waves are not so high as those of the Pacific, whose winds, though less powerful, have a much greater fetch. The very largest waves, about sixty feet high and hundreds of yards long, form in the ' Roaring Forties ' of the southern ocean, where the winds sweep round the world with practically an unlimited fetch.

A growing wave soon becomes too high for its length, its slopes steepening until its face, its foremost slope, is no longer stable. Its crest then overbalances and forms a mass of foam, a *white-cap*, from which the wind tears a shower of spray, the *spindrift*.

This reduces the wave's height, but meanwhile it has grown longer, so that before its crest again overbalances it can rise higher than before. So the waves mount ever higher and spread farther apart, and move faster, until their speed may equal that of the wind.

## WAVE-TRAINS

Very seldom is the wind steady ; it usually varies in direction and force. It then produces several distinct *wave-trains*, groups of similar waves, each group having its own wave length, height, direction and speed, and all mingling to produce a confused choppy sea. Though the whole wave-train travels across the sea in the direction of the wind, it travels only about half as fast as the waves of which it consists.

**Plate 3** Raised beach near Lydstep, Pembrokeshire (p. 75).

One wave-train may overtake another. Then the two sets of waves may reinforce each other, making the crests unusually high and the troughs unusually low; or the crests of one set may coincide with the troughs of the other, producing a short-lived patch of fairly smooth water. When travelling in different directions, conflicting wave-trains combine to produce individual waves of exceptional height.

Though large waves travel faster than smaller ones, they lose strength more quickly. There used to be a superstition that every seventh wave is higher than the other six, but there is no foundation for this. On the other hand a succession of several large waves is likely to be followed by a series of smaller ones.

## OCEAN SWELLS AND TSUNAMI

Waves may outstrip or outlive the wind which produced them, and travel on, even in calm weather, as a *ground swell*. Arriving without any wind to herald them, they can be very dangerous.

An especially dangerous wave or series of waves may be produced by an earthquake either near the coast or on the sea-floor. The waves caused by the Chilean earthquake of 1960 were five miles wide and crossed the Pacific with a speed of about 500 miles an hour, inflicting great damage on the oceanic islands and the coast of Japan. Such waves are sometimes incorrectly called 'tidal waves'; as there is no English name for them they are referred to as *tsunami*, a Japanese term meaning 'large waves in harbours'.

Though the waves out at sea look like a headlong rush of the water, they are in fact little more than an alternate rise and fall of its surface. Floating objects—driftwood, seaweed, patches of foam, or resting sea-birds—are not swept along by the waves but are simply raised and lowered as the ridges of water pass beneath. The waves suggest those which cross a wind-swept cornfield as the blades bow before the gusts and rise after them.

At the crest of the wave each drop moves forward in the same direction as the wind, but it at once swerves downward in a circular course. Its movement becomes vertical, and then, in the trough, it actually moves against the wind. Still continuing the circular course, it swerves upward until it is moving vertically ; arriving at the top of the next crest, it again travels in the wind's direction. Though its movement resembles that of a point on the rim of a revolving wheel, it is not

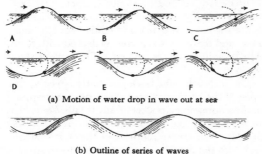

A    B    C

D    E    F

(a) Motion of water drop in wave out at sea

(b) Outline of series of waves

Fig. 2.

circular but a slightly flattened oval; the outline of a series of waves is a cycloidal curve, resembling that traced out by the point as the wheel travels along. (*See* Fig. 2.)

Although the waves do not advance bodily, they do in fact move very slowly in the direction of the wind; they have been compared to a driving-wheel skidding on a slippery road or rail. They may then accelerate the speed of a moving boat, making it travel slightly faster with the waves than it would over a calm sea. Normally, however, this movement is negligible.

## WAVES IN SHALLOW WATER

The circular motion of the water drops extends some distance below the surface, lessening as the depth increases until it peters out, and in shallow water this motion is checked by friction with the sea-floor. This alters the wave's character completely: it becomes shorter, while its height is unaltered, so that its slopes steepen. Its face, being in shallower water than the rearward slope, is the steeper of the two, and tends to overbalance. Here and there the wave-crest is flecked with foam, which rapidly spreads along it. The wave is about to *break*.

On a beach which slopes fairly steeply, the crest of the breaking waves overhangs; entrapping and compressing a pocket of air, it falls, somewhat in advance of the rest of the wave, as a *plunging breaker*. On a more gentle slope the crest sharpens but does not actually overhang: the foam spreads down over the face of the wave, forming a *spilling*

**Plate 4** Chalk cliffs near Cuckmere Haven, Sussex (p. 55).

*breaker*. The splash of the foaming water, the thud of the compressed air released by a plunging breaker, and the grinding of the wave-swept shingle all combine to produce a roar like thunder or like the trampling of countless hoofs—the ' Neptune's white horses ' of our childhood.

Here, in the shallows, the waves—unlike those in the open sea—become an actual shorewards rush of the water, carrying with them driftwood and seaweed and patches of foam, and smiting whatever they strike with some violence. The water from the broken wave surges up the beach with diminishing speed, a movement expressively called the *swash*. This ends as a fan-shaped layer of water and flotsam and foam, or as a wavelet with a miniature crest, or as a succession of two or three such wavelets.

On an open beach that slopes gently enough to produce spilling breakers *surf-riding* is possible. Prone on his surf-board, the rider launches himself just ahead of a suitable wave, preferably one just on the point of breaking. Then he slides down its sloping face, but as the wave keeps pace with him he is, so to speak, sliding down a moving hill. The art of surf-riding is to check the tendency of the unequal pressure of the waves to make the board slew round parallel with them, and to keep it heading for the beach.

## BACKWASH, UNDERTOW AND RIP

Its force spent, the wave retreats seawards, leaving its *reach* marked by a jagged line of seaweed and foam ; this retrograde motion is its *backwash.* Part of its water moves seawards beneath the advancing waves as the *undertow*.

Part of the water, however, moves along parallel to the beach, scouring out a groove beyond which is a *bar*, a ridge of shingle or sand. Where there is a gap in this ridge the water sweeps violently seawards as a *rip*. It is this rip and not, as is commonly supposed, the undertow which endangers a bather who gets caught in it; fortunately it is not very wide, and he should get out of it fairly easily by swimming not towards the beach but parallel with it.

## OBLIQUE WAVES

When a wave drives obliquely towards the beach, its end reaches the shallows first. This shorewards end slows down, while the rest of the wave sweeps on unchecked; and the further inshore the wave advances, the further does this slowing effect spread along it. This slews the wave round so that when it breaks it is, if not actually parallel to the shore, at any rate less oblique to it than are the waves out at sea. Waves sweeping into a bay similarly swerve round to form graceful curves almost parallel to the shoreline. Where a beach consists of alternate ridges and troughs perpendicular to the shore, the waves swerve towards the centre lines of the ridges.

Where the waves arrive obliquely to the beach, their slantwise movement continues after they break into the swash, but it has little effect on the backwash, which retreats down the beach's slope. The water thus travels in a series of un-symmetrical letter V's pointing up the beach.

## REFLECTED AND INTERLACING WAVES : CLAPOTIS

When they encounter a vertical sea-wall, the waves do not necessarily break ; they simply recoil from its surface and travel back seawards. The wall in fact *reflects* them, much as a mirror reflects the waves of light and an echoing cliff those of sound. Two sets of waves then cross the sea in opposite directions.

When two of these wave-crests meet, they do not smash into clouds of spray. There is no reason why they should, for they are not con-flicting masses of moving water, but simply two independent undulations of the surface. They combine momentarily to form a lofty crest, about twice as high as the others, separating two especially deep troughs ; then they pass on unchecked. Here, therefore, the water is un-usually turbulent.

Where the sea-wall is washed by deep water, its action on the waves may be quite different. The retreating waves may then synchronize so accur-ately with the advancing ones that they form a series of *clapotis*. These standing waves do not move across the surface ; the water which forms them alternately rises and falls in the same place. Between the clapotis are *nodes*, stretches of water which remain almost motionless, seemingly unaffected by the turmoil on either side.

When the waves advance obliquely against a sea-wall they recoil at the same angle but slant away in the opposite direction. The two sets of waves then combine to produce an ever-changing pattern of lozenges and squares formed by the moving crests. Even more complicated is the pattern formed by a curved sea-wall.

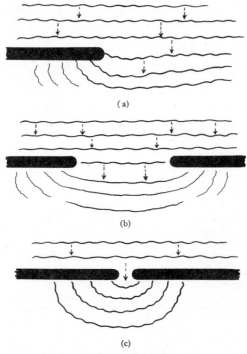

(a)

(b)

(c)

Fig. 3. Waves entering harbour mouths

WAVES ENTERING HARBOUR MOUTHS

When a wave sweeps past the end of a break-water part of it swings round the obstruction to follow a curved course ; this part of the wave loses height, while the remainder drives on unaltered. Each end of a wave entering a *wide* harbour mouth behaves similarly ; so that while sweeping on into the harbour the main wave also sends smaller waves outwards to left and right (Fig. 3(*a*) and (*b*) ).

Very different is the result when the wave enters a *narrow* harbour mouth, a gap shorter than its own length. It then spreads out in all directions within the harbour as a semicircular wave whose height is much the same throughout (Fig. 3(*c*) ).

## WAVES ON ROCKY SHORES

A wave advancing gently against a rugged shoreline adapts itself to the shape of the rocks, recoiling from vertical surfaces, splashing among the boulders, flowing up inclines and into depressions and crannies. It forms numerous rivulets, here slowing down, there advancing more rapidly up a converging channel ; it flows off into side channels, produces tiny cascades and waterfalls, and isolates some of the boulders and reefs.

On an uneven beach it acts similarly, filling the depressions and isolating the ridges. Entering a pool through two separate channels, the water may cross it in opposite directions as two distinct wavelets. Similarly, a wave that follows a winding

34

channel may flow for a short distance towards the sea.

Driven violently on to a rugged shore, a wave smashes into clouds of spray, which may hurtle on faster than the wave itself, even reaching a speed of over 250 feet a second. Carried inland by the wind, the finely divided spray makes the air feel damp and taste salty.

A wave rushing into a tapering cavern that opens inland emerges as a violent and noisy jet of water, air and spray, producing a *blow-hole*; spurting from a blow-hole at the end of a lengthy cavern it may seem to burst mysteriously out of the ground. A blow-hole emerging at the summit of a cliff emits not spray but a gust of air, strong enough to be perceptible and to disturb the grass, and producing an audible ' snort '.

# TIDES

## THE MOON AND THE TIDES

From time immemorial it has been known that the *tides*, the periodical rise and fall of great stretches of water, have something to do with the moon : the usual interval between them, about 12 hours 25 minutes, is roughly half the time the moon takes to circle the earth. Newton explained the tides as being due to the moon's gravitational pull on the water, lifting it to form a bulge resembling an enormous wave-crest. There are in fact two such bulges, one on the side of the earth facing the moon and the other on the earth's far side, for there the moon's pull draws the earth away from the water. Between the two bulges the water is lowered, as though in the troughs between these gigantic wave-crests. (*See* Fig. 4, top.)

Friction between the water and the rotating earth slows the movement of these bulges, so that instead of being exactly beneath the moon they lag a little behind. For this reason *high tide*, as the bulge is called, does not occur exactly when the moon is overhead, but somewhat later.

Were the earth completely surrounded by water, these two progressive waves would for ever travel round it, remaining almost stationary as it revolved beneath them. In fact they get a clear run only in the Antarctic Ocean, from which they send periodical surges of water northwards into the other oceans.

### TIDAL SURGES

Though these progressive waves have to be taken into account in considering the tides, they do not explain them completely. While most shores have two high tides every day, some have only one, and some have none at all. Moreover, broad stretches of inland water, such as the Great Lakes of America, which are unaffected by the ocean's movements, nevertheless have small tides, called *seiches*.

Each of these lakes has its own natural period in which its water surges back and forth to produce the seich, the period depending partly on its length and partly on its depth : the longer and

**Plate 5** *Above :* Waves sweeping in at Pentire Headland, Newquay.
*Below :* Wave breaking over rocky coast, Newquay.

**Plate 6** *Above :* Waves in deep water (p. 27).
*Below :* Wave ripples crossing (p. 32).

shallower it is, the shorter is its period. If a lake's natural period roughly equals the tidal interval of about $12\frac{1}{2}$ hours, the surge is much more strongly marked.

Similar surges are formed in the sea, whose water fills a number of depressions varying in size and depth. Each of these depressions has its own natural surge-period, but each is affected not only by the moon's gravitational pull on its own water, but also by the behaviour of the water in the adjoining depressions. This makes the calculation of the water's movements very difficult; it has to be carried out by special *tide-predicting machines*.

## LOCAL TIDES

Hence instead of one great progressive tide circling the earth, there are a number of local tides, differing greatly in the areas they cover. These tides, moreover, are affected by the earth's rotation, so that instead of merely surging to and fro they circle round centres, the *amphidromic points*, where the water is almost stationary and there is hardly any tide at all. They do not sweep bodily round these points like a huge whirlpool; they simply form an immense wave which circles around them—counter-clockwise in the northern hemisphere—producing a rhythmic rise and fall of the water's surface.

One immense wave traverses the North Atlantic, the tide rising round the British Isles as it falls off the eastern coast of Canada, and vice versa. A smaller wave in the North Sea sends a tide southwards down the coast of East Anglia and northwards up that of Holland. Other local tides are formed off Denmark ; off southern Norway ; between Northern Ireland and the Mull of Kintyre ; between northern Scotland and Iceland ; and in the Caribbean Sea.

Tideless regions exist not only near the amphidromic points but where two adjacent tides conflict so that the rise of the one counteracts the fall of the other. Conversely, where two such tides reinforce one another the rise and fall of the water is especially marked.


## SPRING AND NEAP TIDES

The sun's gravitational pull similarly raises tides akin to, but less powerful than, those caused by the moon. Their period is about twelve hours instead of about twelve and a half, and the two interact. At full and new moon, when the sun and moon are in a straight line with the earth—this recurs at intervals of about a fortnight—they co-operate to produce an especially powerful *spring tide*,[1] which rises higher and falls lower than usual ; at the first and third quarters, when they form a right angle with the earth—again roughly at fortnightly intervals—their pulls conflict, making a *neap tide* whose range is unusually small. (*See* Fig. 4.)

---

[1] This has nothing to do with the annual season. The spring tides occur throughout the year.

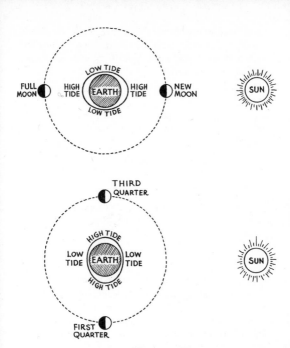

Fig. 4. Spring and neap tides

## TIDAL EBB AND FLOW

In mid ocean the tides, like the ordinary waves, are simply a rhythmic rise and fall of the water. On the continental shelf, however, they act like the waves on a beach, and become a bodily rush of the water towards or away from the land. The rising water produces the tide's *flow* or *flood*; its fall is the *ebb*; and between them, when the tide is almost at a standstill, there are brief periods of *slack water*.

When it reaches the shore the tide acts like an enormous wave. Sweeping up the inlets, it converts some of the rocks and sandbanks into islets and others into *shoals*—shallows hidden beneath the water. Following the windings of the inlets, the rising tide may flow parallel to, or even towards, the shoreline. It turns depressions on the beach into lagoons which broaden and deepen and at last merge into the sea. To get caught by the rising tide on an isolated rock or sandbank, or at the foot of an unscalable cliff, is one of the perils of the seashore.

## TIDAL WAVES AND RACES

A tapering river mouth may convert the rising tide into a *tidal wave*, known locally as an *eagre* or *bore*. Crowded together by the converging banks, the surging water becomes a powerful wave whose face steepens, overhangs, and collapses into a roaring wall of surf; in the River Severn it may be several feet high. Though dangerous it is easy to avoid, for the time of its possible arrival can be predicted; and unless conditions are favourable the tidal wave may completely fail to develop.

The more gently the floor of an inlet slopes, the faster the rising tide sweeps up it. In an estuary whose bed changes abruptly from a steep slope near its mouth to a more gentle incline further along, the tide creeps forward insidiously until it reaches the place where the slope changes ; then it makes a sudden—and very dangerous— forward rush.

A tide sweeping up a long narrow sea channel is especially powerful. The highest tides in the world are those which sweep, like a bore fifty feet high, through the Bay of Fundy, between New Brunswick and Nova Scotia.

In channels broken by rocks and shallows, such as the Menai Straits, the tide swirls and froths in dangerous *overfalls*. In such places, and where two tides meet, as off the north coast of Scotland, there may be a dangerous *tidal race*, a swift rush of the water, also called a *tide-rip* or *rip-tide*. There are places, too, where the tide forms whirlpools, and of these two have passed into legend : the Maelstrom off northern Norway, and Charybdis in the Gulf of Messina.

# CURRENTS

### RIVERS OF THE SEA

Seasonal changes in temperature, as the summer warmth makes the water expand and the chill of winter makes it contract, combine with the winds to keep the oceans in continual movement. *Currents*, like immense rivers, traverse the seas, and the earth's rotation diverts their flow : towards the right in the northern hemisphere, towards the left in the southern. This converts them into *gyrals*, gigantic whirlpools, which are broken by counter-currents flowing the opposite way.

Unlike the waves and tides in deep water, but like waves swashing up a beach or tides in shallow water, the currents actually are progressive movements of the sea. They flow with a spiral or corkscrew motion and bring to the surface water from the depths, laden with the material which living creatures need.

## THE GULF STREAM

In the North Atlantic, trade winds blowing from the north-east send the North Equatorial Current moving westwards. The islands in the Caribbean Sea, and the Isthmus of Panama, deflect it first northwards and then eastwards, converting it into the Florida Current, which flows right across the Atlantic as the Gulf Stream.

The western coast of Europe splits the flow of the water, diverting part of it south as the Canaries Stream to rejoin the North Equatorial Current. Within the gyral thus produced masses of weed accumulate : south of the Bermudas they form the Sargasso Sea inhabited by interesting creatures unknown elsewhere.

## THE NORTH ATLANTIC DRIFT

The rest of the Stream broadens and flows more slowly towards Europe as the *North Atlantic Drift*. It then divides into several smaller currents. One flows along the coast of Ireland, northern Scotland, and Norway, sending a side stream southwards into the North Sea ; approaching the

**Plate 7**  *Above :*  Waves breaking over submerged rocks, Cornish coast.
*Below :*  Waves breaking on shallow beach near Newquay, Cornwall.

**Plate 8** High and low tide levels at St. Helier Harbour, Jersey.

Baltic, this stream swings round and rejoins the main drift off the Norwegian coast. Another flows northwards up the Irish Sea. Another travels eastwards up the English Channel and

Fig. 5. Course of the Gulf Stream

through the Straits of Dover into the North Sea. (*See* Fig. 5.)

These currents do not flow steadily; like rivers of the land they have their eddies and backwaters, and they are subdivided and deflected by the headlands. When unusually powerful they so to speak overflow and send off temporary side streams; one, branching off from the current in the Irish Sea, flows southwards from Cardigan Bay round Pembrokeshire into the Bristol Channel.

## CURRENTS AND TIDES

The currents combine with the tides to produce important effects on the flow of water. When, round the British Isles, the two act together and are perhaps urged on by the westerly wind, they drive the water up-Channel much more rapidly than the falling tide, working against the current, can bring it down. Thus in the long run the current acts almost as effectively as if the tides had not been there.

## DEEP OCEAN CURRENTS

During the recent International Geophysical Year new methods were devised of investigating the depths of the sea. These revealed the existence of *deep ocean currents* well below the surface. Though much remains to be learned about them, they are already known to be very complicated. One, immediately below the Gulf Stream, flows in the opposite direction from the Stream itself; and, as might have been expected, it moves much more slowly, for it is checked by friction with the sea-floor, whereas the Stream is helped by the prevailing wind. These gradual deep-sea water-flows have far-reaching results which demand further study.

48

# THE SEASHORE

## COASTAL EROSION

### BETWEEN THE TIDES

The *high-water mark*, the limit reached by the rising tide, is obvious almost all round the coast, but there is of course no corresponding *low-water mark*—it would be concealed by the sea. In the *intertidal zone* between them the work of the sea is obvious, and it can be traced in the *splash zone*, above high tide but within reach of the spray.

On the beaches the high-water mark is shown by a line of material left by the retreating waves. In the intertidal zone the irregularities in the sand are erased or smoothed, its mounds being flattened, its depressions partly filled in, and its slopes made more gentle ; and the sand itself becomes plastic enough to retain impressions of anything that touches it. It is traversed by ripple marks caused by movement of the water below the surface (Fig. 6) ; it is pitted with rain-prints ; larger pits, and string-like tangles of damp sand near by, indicate the lurking-place of marine worms. Footprints mark the trails of animals or birds, and vague scrapings those of more lowly animals, or the contact of seaweed fronds. (Such impressions are usually

Fig. 6. Ripple marks on sand

erased by the tide, but some remained while the beaches hardened to form sandstone, and have honorary rank as fossils.)

Along the cliffs the high-water mark may be indicated by a line of lichens, making the rocks look from a distance as if a horizontal line had been ruled across them. Below this they are discoloured by the brine, and their surfaces are smoothed and their edges rounded by material rasped against them by the waves. They are festooned with seaweed, studded with shell-fish and honeycombed by rock-boring animals.

### 'SHAKER OF EARTH'

The waves, which consist of tons of water hurled violently and almost incessantly against the shore, do far more than level the sand and discolour the rocks. The Greeks of old called the god of the sea the ' Earth Shaker ' ; and earthquake-recording instruments indeed show that the waves literally make the ground tremble.

During the winter they are incredibly powerful. They tear across the beaches and leap against the cliffs, sea-walls and piers ; they have wrenched apart the massive blocks of an esplanade, tons in weight and clamped together. They assault the cliffs not merely with their own impetus but with boulders like battering-rams, pebbles like projectiles, and masses of sand like an abrasive powder.

They drive the air before them and compress it against the cliff face ; when released it expands violently with almost an explosive effect, weakening and ripping away part of the cliff. Still more destructive does the air become when it is forced into the rock crevices, compressed, and then left free to expand. Thus the waves destroy the cliffs, undermining them until their upper part collapses.

## WEATHER ACTION

The sea's destructiveness is aided by that of the weather. Alternately heated and cooled by changes in temperature, the surface of the rocks expands and contracts, and its loosened fragments fall away. The wind pelts the rocks with grit like a sand-blast. Rain and sea water not only dissolve certain types of rock but penetrate into the crevices ; and when water freezes in winter it

**Plate 9** Drowned valley, Porth Clais, near St. David's, Pembrokeshire (p. 74).

expands irresistibly. So, both below and above tide level, the face of the cliff is slowly worn away.

# COASTAL TYPES

## CLAY AND SAND

Each type of rock is differently affected by wave and weather. Cliffs of loose sand and gravel, such as the *crags* of East Anglia, are easily destroyed not only by large waves but by the incessant swirling of the sea. Clay when damp becomes slippery and may slide seawards like a glacier of mud ; when dry it hardens and develops cracks which widen and deepen until a whole cliff face may collapse bodily.

## SANDSTONE AND CONGLOMERATE

The structure of the harder bedded rocks, which consist of parallel layers of grains or pebbles cemented together, is in itself a source of weakness. Sandstone and conglomerate are divided by *bedding-planes* parallel to, and *joints* perpendicular to, their layers. Along these planes and joints, and indeed wherever these rocks are softer and more loosely cemented than elsewhere, the sea readily attacks them. Working its way into the cliffs, it excavates caves and gullies separated by projecting buttresses ; cutting in behind the buttresses, it converts them into towering island *stacks* ; finally, undercutting the stacks, it overthrows them.

Where the layers of rock dip (slope) inland the cliff is fairly stable. It is more quickly destroyed when they dip seaward, for then the loosened material is apt to slide down the sloping surface of the layer below into the sea.

The Old Red Sandstone of Caithness is penetrated by caves and blow-holes and by *goes* or *geos*, deep narrow inlets formed where the sea cut inland along a joint or a cave roof collapsed. Even some of the stacks are undermined so that they stand, table fashion, on four corner ' legs '.

Movements of the rock and variations in its colour produce unusual scenic effects. On the Pembrokeshire coast, for example, some of the rocks have been turned bodily on end, and the colours range from greenish grey to red.

## LIMESTONE AND CHALK

Limestone, like sandstone, is a bedded rock, and it too has planes and joints along which the sea can penetrate. Unlike the sandstone it is slightly soluble, and the brine slowly dissolves its surface. It is also tunnelled with caverns and crevices formed by the rivers, which the sea can enter and enlarge. Limestone cliffs therefore abound in caves, blow-holes and inlets, and are abundantly fringed by reefs and stacks.

Chalk, akin to limestone but far softer, is attacked more rapidly by weather and sea. Though having few natural caves, it develops weaknesses not only along its joints and bedding-planes but wherever the surface water seeps into it. It forms steep, almost vertical, cliffs, diversified by chasms and buttresses and detached stacks and reefs.

Where earth movements tilt the chalk so that its layers are vertical, they compress and harden it and make it more resistant than elsewhere to the sea's attack. This hardened chalk forms the ' backbone ' of the Isle of Wight, a ridge from east to west which was once continuous with the chalk of Purbeck. The intervening portion has been destroyed by the sea, its vestiges forming a picturesque line of stacks, the Needles.

## GRANITE AND BASALT

Rocks which are not divided into layers are harder than the bedded rocks and more resistant : the Land's End granite braves the fierce Atlantic gales. Granite is, however, traversed by joints and cracks, many of them irregular, forming lines of weakness along which the sea can act. In the Scilly Isles and elsewhere this *mural* jointing gives it a castellated appearance, resembling masonry.

Basalt forms narrow layers which, when the softer-bedded rocks have been worn away around them, stand out as capes or islands. The Great Whin Sill, a bold ridge in the north of England, forms the headlands of Bamburgh and Dunstanburgh and the Farne Islands.

Basalt also occurs in larger masses. In the Giant's Causeway of Northern Ireland and in the Isle of Staffa its contraction in cooling has given it a

**Plate 10**  Coastline near Treen, Cornwall.

strange columnar formation, consisting of upright prisms of rock fitting closely together. The sea has pierced Staffa with a number of caverns, the best known being Fingal's Cave.

## COMPOSITE SHORELINES

Where different types of rock lie side by side, the sea destroys them unequally, producing a diversified coastline. The softer rocks yield quickly, forming bays and coves and inlets separated by headlands built of the more resistant materials.

Where the soft rocks underlie the hard, their destruction may produce a landslip, the upper layers being undermined until they subside bodily seawards. Their remains form the Landslip west of Lyme Regis, the Warren near Folkestone, the Isle of Wight Undercliff and many smaller masses of foundered material.

The Blue Lias rock-beds east of Lyme Regis consist of alternate horizontal layers of hard limestone and soft shale. As the soft shale is eroded the harder slabs fall away, producing minor landslips and strewing the shore with fallen material.

The rock-beds in the ' Isle ' of Purbeck are vertical, the great inland mass of chalk being separated from the coast by narrow beds first of clay and then of limestone, both tapering from east to west. Here several stages of the sea's destructive action are visible. At Stair Hole it has cut through the limestone and attacked the

57

clay, forming a conical funnel-shaped cavity. At Lulworth Cove the limestone has been widely breached, and the destruction of the clay has resulted in a circular inlet of great beauty. To the west the limestone has been reduced to a line of offshore reefs, the clay has gone completely, and the sea is now attacking the chalk. Further along the coast a resistant mass of limestone, formerly continuous with that of Purbeck, remains as the Isle of Portland.

## RIVER MOUTHS

Where a river reaches the sea the two combine to destroy the land. With the larger rivers the result is a broad estuary or a delta of several channels. The smaller streams fall as a cascade over the harder rocks or cut channels, such as the chines of the Isle of Wight, into the softer materials. Where a stream flows parallel to the coast the sea may cut a ravine into its channel and intercept its waters, leaving the lower part of its bed as a dry valley a little way inland.

## LOST LANDS

Apart from occasional spectacular landslips or other inroads of the sea, the destruction of the coast is so gradual that it goes almost unnoticed. In the aggregate, however, as the ancient maps and records show plainly, it is far-reaching. Thousands of acres of soil, with many villages and several flourishing towns, have vanished from the British coast.

Seaton and Ravenspur, on the north-east coast of England; Old Winchelsea and Brighthelmstone, the forerunner of Brighton, in the south— these former towns have been destroyed with the countryside around them. East Anglia once extended into the North Sea beyond Lowestoft. Nor is the process at an end, for the sea is still attacking the coast; but for such artificial protections as the sea-walls east of Brighton and on the north coast of Kent, the destruction would be greater still.

# SEABORNE SANDS AND SHINGLE

## COLLAPSED MATERIAL

The sea attacks not merely the face of the cliffs but the debris piled up at their feet. The loose material is soon swept away by the waves. The larger fragments, too heavy for them to move, meet the brunt of the sea's attack, and for a time protect the land from further destruction.

In doing so they themselves are destroyed. The waves jostle them together and grind against them the smaller fragments and the grains of sand, blunting their angles and smoothing their surfaces. So the large rock masses become rounded boulders and the smaller become pebbles, while much sand and silt is worn from their surface. Gradually the boulders are worn down, while the pebbles either become small enough for the sea to wash away or are reduced to sand. At last the bulk of the material is destroyed and the sea then attacks the cliffs anew.

**Plate II**  Southern dip in Ridgeway Conglomerate, Angle, Pembrokeshire (p. 53).

The waves also grind the pebbles and sand against the sea-floor, smoothing its irregularities and slowly wearing it away. Eddies in the water rotate the pebbles, which act like boring tools, piercing the rock with shallow rounded holes. Revealed at low tide, these depressions can be recognized by their rounded shape and their smooth surface ; lying in them may be the pebbles which formed them and which will enlarge and smooth them when the sea again swirls them about.

This process flattens the rocky shore at the foot of the cliff and converts it into a *wave-cut platform* with a gentle seawards slope. Its surface is not quite regular, for it may consist of different types of rock, and the waves which attack it vary in direction and form.

The typical *shore profile* is thus a steep cliff from whose foot this platform, of bare rock or with a surface covering of sand or shingle, slopes gently down to and beyond the sea. As the waves cut the cliff further back the platform broadens.

## EFFECTS OF TIDES AND CURRENT

Most of the material worn from cliff face and platform is sooner or later swept away by the moving water, and the faster this moves the heavier the fragments it can dislodge. Flowing swiftly, it carries away pebbles as well as silt, but as its flow slackens it deposits most of them on the sea-floor : first pebbles, in order of size, then the sand and lastly the silt. It thus sorts the material out roughly by size and weight, mingled as it is with sand and silt and shell fragments from the sea-floor.

Moving more swiftly when current and tides work together than when they are opposed, the sea transports the material more effectively with the current than against it : northwards up the Irish Sea, southwards down the North Sea, eastwards along the English Channel. Material from the cliffs of Cornwall may be washed ashore near the Straits of Dover.

## FORMATION OF BEACHES

In the shallows friction with the sea-floor slows the water, which at once begins to deposit the material it carries. The wave-cut platform then becomes a *beach* of shingle or sand, mingled with fragments of sea-shell. Some of the beaches extend for miles along the coast, but most of them occur in bays and inlets, which check the flow of the water. Round the headlands this moves so swiftly that, far from depositing loose material, it actually sweeps it away.

As the swash from a breaking wave moves faster than the backwash, more material travels up the beach than down. On some beaches the coarser material piles up in a ridge near high-tide level ; on others the pebbles are simply left higher up the beach than the sand, which is swept seawards by the backwash.

Elsewhere the material is sorted out not up the beach but along it. On the Chesil Bank of Dorset, a long shingle beach, the grading is remarkable; very small at its western end, near Bridport, the pebbles are quite large at its eastern end, near Portland. The reasons for this are conjectural; by sheltering the western part of the Bank, Start Point may deflect the sea's flow eastward.

The zigzag flow of water from waves driven obliquely shorewards by the wind gives a sideways movement to the material they carry, the whole beach having a *longshore drift* in the same direction as the prevailing wind. This, together with the movement of the sand and shingle swept along by the currents, has to be artificially checked by the *groynes*, walls built perpendicularly down the beach. The difference in level of the beaches on the opposite sides of the groyne gives striking evidence of the strength of the longshore drift.

### BARS, QUICKSANDS AND SPITS

Where a river meets the rising tide, they check one another's flow; each deposits much of the material it carries, the silt of the river mingling with the seaborne sand. Small streams crossing a beach simply form a tract of slimy mud. In the estuaries the river flow combines with the scour of the ebbing tide to sweep the deposited material harmlessly out to sea. Failing this the mud may accumulate so much as to impede navigation; then it has to be artificially dredged up and removed.

When the material accumulates somewhat off-shore it forms a *harbour bar* across the river mouth,

Plate 12    The Green Bridge of Wales, Pembrokeshire, a natural arch
cut in carboniferous limestone (p. 54).

its presence being revealed by the surf which breaks along it. A bar, especially in bad weather, can be as dangerous as a submerged reef.

Deposited by the tide as its flow slackens, or scooped up from a shallow sea-floor by the waves, a similar ridge may accumulate somewhat out to sea as an *offshore bar*. When this consists of very fine sand or silt, saturated with water and rendered slimy by clay, it forms the deadly *quicksand*, which inexorably sucks down and stifles anyone who ventures upon it.

The longshore drift of a beach, or the growth of a bar, may completely block the mouth of a stream. Some of the water thus impounded seeps through the sand or between the pebbles and accumulates behind them to form a marsh or lagoon. Dammed by the Loe Bar, the Caher Stream near Helston forms the Loe Pool, and behind the Chesil Bank are several pools, including the long narrow Fleet.

Instead of blocking the mouth of a river, a bar may simply divert its flow. The eastward course of the River Alde in Suffolk has been diverted southwards by a bar which within historical times has grown several miles and which might have been even longer had it not been curtailed more than once by storms.

The material the sea deposits may form not a bar parallel to the land but a *spit* jutting out from it : Spurn Head, in Yorkshire, well shows the tendency of the spits to end in a hook, formed where the shoals divert the waves. The spit may later extend beyond the hook and then produce another hook, or even several; these become laterals (side ridges)—there are several of them on the bank of shingle near Hurst Castle in Hampshire, at the western end of the Solent.

Spits, bars and beaches may be partly destroyed by a storm, and then accumulate anew. Or they may be rebuilt almost as quickly as they are destroyed. Others are permanent, the wave-borne material fringing the shore as an intermediate region between the sea and the actual land. The bulk removal of sand or shingle from the foreshore may have to be prohibited, as it would lead to harmful destruction of the coast. A sand beach is not merely a playground for the children and a holiday haunt for adults: in many places it protects the land from the onslaught of the waves.

In recent times the appearance of many stretches of beach has been greatly affected by the discharge from oil-tankers of waste material from their tanks. Carried inshore by movements of the sea, this forms patches of tar, not merely unsightly but very noxious to the life of the coast. It is very difficult to remove or destroy, and though it may be covered by movements of the shingle or sand, further movements may bring it once more to the surface.

## LAND RECLAMATION

### Sand dunes

Dry sand grains are so light that the wind can blow them away. Dropped during a lull, or checked by obstacles, they pile up as the *dunes*, wave-like ridges and mounds of sand. On their windward side the dunes are convex, and on their lee they are concave; a steady wind drives their ends forward, giving them a crescent shape, but variable winds convert them into shapeless heaps or merge them into a chaos of ridges.

The wind-blown sand grains may travel far inland. Covering the fields, choking or diverting the streams, piling up against obstacles, the drifting sand has buried whole buildings and transformed fertile land into a small desert. In Cornwall, East Anglia and South Wales, and in Moray Firth, it has done widespread damage, and in the Landes of Gascony it has been more destructive still.

Fortunately the drift can be checked, and the dunes immobilized, by the artificial planting of *marram grass*, a plant so hardy that it can find nourishment even in the sand. The grass spreads over the surface and protects it against the wind, while its roots spread below, forming an underlying network which binds the sand.

The grass also fertilizes the dune so that sea-spurge and sea-holly can grow upon it, to be followed by lichens and convolvulus (bindweed). Rabbits burrow into the dune and they too fertilize it with organic material. Slowly the whitish sand becomes a brownish-grey soil.

Wherever this surface covering is removed the wind acts anew, scooping an excavation in the sand, undercutting the vegetation, and perhaps driving a gully right through the dune and building another dune to its lee. Then the grass and its successors gradually re-cover the exposed surface and bind the newly formed dune.

Judicious planting of marram grass has checked the drift of tracts of moving sand and enabled it to be transformed into plantations. Thus the threatened Landes of Gascony have been saved and extensive afforestation schemes have prospered on the shores of Moray Firth.

## THE DEVELOPMENT OF SPITS AND BARS

The waves may wash an offshore bar landwards until it merges with the beach. Tide-washed or wind-blown sand may accumulate between the laterals of a spit, giving the marram grass a foothold, and converting the spit into an island of pebble ridges separated by narrow strips of sandy but fertile soil, which may extend until it touches the shore.

The structure of Scolt Head and Blakeney Point, in Norfolk, shows that they were formerly long spits with several laterals. The one still an island and the other merged with the shore, they are now so rich in plant and animal life that the National Trust protects them as bird sanctuaries.

### SALT-MARSHES

Across a gently sloping beach just below high-water level the tide moves very slowly; and here it readily drops its silt, depositing it against obstacles as trifling as the holdfasts of the seaweed. This produces small patches of mud, and as these further check the flow of the water and make it deposit more of its silt, they gradually grow higher and extend further. They may convert a former beach into a marsh of flattish tracts of mud traversed by shallow water channels.

On the newly formed salt-marsh the seaweeds are first accompanied and then replaced by such hardy land plants as the sea-aster, the sea-pink, the sea-lavender and the common marsh grass, whose seeds are brought to it by the tide, on the wind, by the birds and even—inadvertently—by human visitors. Their growth checks the flow of the water and produces a further deposit of silt on to which the vegetation can spread. At last much of the marsh may rise just above sea level and the seaweeds be completely replaced by land plants ; what was once a beach is now a tract of low-lying pasture-land.

By the systematic draining of the marshes and the construction of dikes to bar out the sea, the process is accelerated. Except in the brackish ditches the salt-loving plants are replaced by docks, thistles and nettles, diversified with butter-cups and daisies. The former salt-marsh is now fit for cultivation : it has been reclaimed from the sea.

### RECLAIMED LAND

The land reclamation round the Zuyder Zee and elsewhere in Holland is deservedly famous. England too has its Holland, the low-lying shore around the Wash, from which many acres have been reclaimed. Similar work has been done beside the Scottish firths, in the Fenlands of East Anglia and Yorkshire, and in Romney Marsh. The rapid growth of a salt-marsh plant, *Spartina townsendii*, has caused much unpremeditated silting up along the south coast of England. Even where, as in Morecambe Bay in Lancashire, the reclaimed land is too sandy for cultivation it can be built on ; part of the sea front of Southport is an example.

Narrow inlets along which the tide moves sluggishly are easily silted up. Thanet, now an island only in name, was once separated from the Kentish mainland by channels in which vessels sought refuge from the gales of the North Sea. The ' islands ' of Axholme south of the Humber and Oxney in Kent are bordered by strips of low-lying land which were once narrow waterways.

Extensive silting up on the south coast has completely cut off from the sea several of the historic Cinque Ports : Sandwich, Old Romney, Winchelsea and Rye.

## DELTAS

Silt brought down by the rivers and deposited when they are checked by the tide accumulates in the larger estuaries to form low-lying stretches of country : examples are the plain beside the lower Thames and the Low Countries (Netherlands) bordering the mouth of the Rhine. Lower Egypt largely consists of masses of silt, traditionally ' the gift of the Nile ' ; and this river crosses them to the sea through a network of channels. Two of the main channels, together with the

**Plate 13**  Coastal erosion of soft cliff face (p. 53).

**Plate 14** *Above :* Waves beating against rocky cliffs at St. Gowan's Head, Pembrokeshire.
*Below :* Old Harry Rocks, Swanage (p. 55).

coastline, form a triangle resembling the Greek letter delta (Δ). This term is therefore used to describe any diverging system of river mouths.

## COASTAL FLOODING

Land reclaimed from the sea is necessarily flattish and low-lying. As certain types of soil shrink when they dry, part of the land, now protected by dikes, may actually be a little *below* sea level. If the sea should breach or overflow the dikes the result is disastrous flooding, with the interruption of communications, the widespread destruction of property and livestock, and the possible loss of human life. By drenching the soil with brine the sea also renders the flooded area unfit for cultivation.

The disastrous floods of early 1953, which swamped much of Holland as well as the east coast of England, were produced by the combination of a very high spring tide, a heavy rainfall resulting in swollen rivers, and a strong wind blowing southwards and driving a storm-surge into the funnel-shaped North Sea.

Though dikes minimize flooding they cannot completely prevent it. Another similar combination of tide, rainfall and wind might cause another more far-reaching storm-surge. It is obviously impracticable to protect the whole of East Anglia with an immense dike ; and even if this were possible the result would simply be to divert the advancing waters into the river mouths and so flood the country from inland.

# EVIDENCE OF EARTH MOVEMENTS

## SUBSIDENCE OF THE LAND

Compared with the restless ever-moving sea the solid earth appears to be changeless and immovable. This, however, is an illusion : there is clear evidence that parts of the coast have sunk bodily, so that what was once dry land is now covered by the waves.

The river mouths in the south of Devon and Cornwall are very different from the usual estuary. Long narrow inlets whose steep banks are clothed down to high tide level with vegetation, they have a striking resemblance to the inland valleys artificially dammed to form reservoirs. Such *drowned valleys*—a Welsh example is Milford Haven, Pembrokeshire—also exist elsewhere in England and on the western coasts of Scotland, Ireland and Norway.

Off the coasts are a number of submerged forests, the remains buried in the sand of trees many of which belong to species that normally grow some distance inland. Beneath the Dogger Bank and elsewhere are submerged peat-bogs and submerged beds of leaf-mould. St. Michael's Mount, near Penzance, has a Cornish name which means ' the ancient rock in the midst of the woods ' : it is now an island connected with the shore only at low tide.

## EMERGENCE OF THE LAND

Other parts of the coast give equally clear evidence that they have risen out of the sea.

A shore profile normally characteristic of the actual coast, with its cliff towering over the wave-cut platform, occurs a little distance inland and well above sea level. In places on the Scottish coast two, or even three, of these *raised beaches* are situated one above the other, at heights of from 25 to 100 feet above high tide.

## RECENT EARTH MOVEMENTS

Similar *earth movements* have taken place in fairly recent times. A few, caused by earthquakes, have been sudden: in 1855 part of the New Zealand coast rose about 9 feet. Others have been gradual and more difficult to detect, but there is direct evidence of at least one. Over two hundred years ago marks were made, on a calm day, at sea level on the coast of the tideless Baltic. They are now so far above sea level as to indicate that since they were made the eastern coast of Sweden has risen about 9 inches in the south, and about 36 inches towards the north, per century.

## SUBSIDENCE AND RE-EMERGENCE

Many rocks show evidence of more than one change of level. *Fossil forests*, in which tree roots and trunks have been transformed into stone, such as those on the cliff edge near Lulworth Cove, indicate this double movement: the trees, which grew on dry land, had to sink beneath the sea to become 'petrified', and they have since risen above it.

The very structure of the bedded rocks shows that they were formed beneath the waves. Chalk resembles a hardened ooze from the sea-floor, shale a hardened mud-flat, sandstone a hardened beach and conglomerate a hardened pebble bed. Some rocks, moreover, teem with fossils : there are limestones consisting largely of fossil seaweeds, corals or shell-fish. Only powerful earth movements could have raised them above the sea.

Clearly, then, the coast has undergone far-reaching changes. Not only have tracts of land been destroyed by the waves and others been formed by the accumulation of silt, but, not once or twice but several times, the earth has swayed bodily up and down. The land has sunk beneath the sea ; the sea-floor has risen and hardened to form dry land.

Similarities in the structure of the cliffs on the two sides of the English Channel show that Britain was once united to the Continent by an isthmus : the borings made by marine animals may have helped the sea to destroy it.

It is now widely believed that the general ' parallelism ' of the two shores of the Atlantic indicates that America was once united to western Europe and Africa, but that it was split off and thrust bodily thousands of miles away by earth movements.

Such considerations add credence to the ancient legends of inhabited lands swamped by the sea within historic times. According to one tradition, the Cartref-y-Gwaelod, described as ' that most

**Plate 15**  Rock formation at Stair Hole, adjoining Lulworth Cove, Dorset (p. 58).

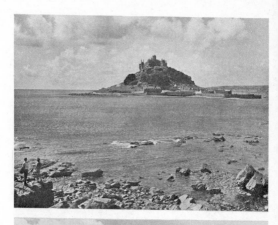

**Plate 16** *Above :* St. Michael's Mount, Cornwall (p. 74).
*Below :* Giant's Causeway, Northern Ireland (p. 55).

beautiful, fertile and pleasant vale', is now the 'Lost Hundred' submerged by the waters of Cardigan Bay. According to another a mighty forest, where King Arthur and his knights and ladies used to hunt, near Tintagel in Cornwall, has now become the 'Lost Land of Lyonesse' with only a few of its hills remaining above the Atlantic; they are now the Scilly Isles.

# SOME SEASHORE SIGHTS

## In the sky

The sea horizon gives scope for observing sights in the heavens difficult to notice inland. Towards nightfall a vague darkness may sometimes be seen rising slowly in the east: this is the *shadow of the earth*, cast by the setting sun upon the air. At the last gleam of sunset the famous *green ray* may flash upwards from the skyline: whoever catches a glimpse of this 'living light' will, so tradition runs, never be deceived in matters affecting the heart!

A brightness above the horizon below which the sun has set is the *afterglow*; its counterpart, visible in the east a little before sunrise, is the *false dawn*, the two forming the *zodiacal light*. During the night a faintly gleaming circle may cross the sky from east to west; it is the *counter-glow*, moving so as to keep opposite the sun. From Scotland and other northerly regions, though seldom from England, the *Northern Lights* (Aurora Borealis) may be seen flickering in the night sky. These phenomena of course demand a clear sky, and are best seen on moonless nights.

## IN THE AIR

Atmospheric conditions may affect the loom of distant objects, making them seem larger and nearer than they really are. They occasionally produce a *mirage*, a reflection above the horizon of ships or a distant shore hidden below it. Distortion usually makes the reflections unrecognizable, simply giving a general impression of fairy-tale castles and unearthly landscapes.

It may be the influence of the sea's proximity on the refraction of the air which makes the sunlight more intense on the coast than inland, so that the photographer needs a smaller stop, or a shorter exposure, than usual. Here too, for the same reason, there is an increased risk of sunstroke or sunburn.

## IN THE SEA

Icebergs seldom drift near temperate shores. Towering masses of gleaming ice carried along by the tides and currents, they form an impressive spectacle. Only about one-ninth of their bulk is visible, the rest being submerged ; as this portion melts in the water's warmth the berg becomes increasingly top-heavy, and at last overturns dramatically.

Elsewhere the bergs constitute a serious menace to navigation. The International Iceberg Patrol, maintained jointly by the United States and Great Britain, and manned by the U.S. Coastguard, plots the movements of the bergs and warns shipping of their proximity.

**Plate 17** PLANTS OF SHINGLE AND
SANDY FORESHORES

1. Yellow horned poppy, *Glaucium flavum* : 2 ft.  2. Sea-campion, *Silene maritima* : 6 in.  3. Sea-sandwort, *Honckenya peploides* : 9 in.  4. Sea-wormwood, *Artemisia maritima* · 12 in.  5. Sea-bindweed, *Calystegia soldanella* : 12 in.  6. Sea-beet, *Beta maritima* : 2 ft.  7. Orache, *Atriplex patula* : 2 ft.

F

*Water-spouts*, too, are unusual in temperate seas, being more common in the tropics. They resemble small tornadoes : a swirl in the air lifts a column of spray from the sea ; at the same time a column of mist extends downwards from a lowering cloud above, and the two meet to form a rotating pillar of mingled water and mist. Moving slowly across the waves, a large water-spout can endanger shipping, but it seldom lasts long and can be dispersed by gunfire.

On dark nights the surface of the sea may become luminous ; this effect is produced by the combined *phosphorescence* of countless microscopic creatures. Though not so brilliant as that of the glow-worm, their united gleam can be surprisingly bright.

## On ships

*St. Elmo's Fire* is a gleam of electrical origin occasionally visible on the tips of masts and spars. Though it appears in thundery weather, it does not flash out like lightning ; it is a harmless form of static electricity, resembling the brush discharge sometimes produced on electrical apparatus.

## Some ancient legends

The idea of a sea monster resembling a giant serpent was known in Ancient Egypt. Though few naturalists take it seriously, there are several fairly well-corroborated accounts of its appearance, and the late Commander R. T. Gould gave in his book *The Case for the Sea-serpent* evidence for the existence of three distinct types of sea monster unknown to science. One resembles a long-necked seal. Another, the moha-moha, said to appear off New Zealand, resembles a large turtle. The third, possibly akin to the Loch Ness Monster, has a long tail and neck and a massive body which it can raise into humps ; though somewhat suggestive of the extinct plesiosaurus, it may be not a reptile but a mammal.

The reputed existence of an even larger monster is likewise unconfirmed. The *kraken* was said to be so vast that it could be mistaken for an island, and to possess many large squid-like tentacles. Impossible as this sounds, it may have a factual basis : the existence of a giant squid was long ridiculed by the naturalists—until unmistakable fragments of its tentacles came to light.

Whatever the truth about sea-serpent and kraken, it is only their bulk which renders their existence suspect. As the second part of this book will show, they could hardly be more bizarre than the living creatures of the sea and the shore.

# LIVING CREATURES OF SEA AND SEASHORE

## LIFE IN THE SEA

### Variety and interest

The sea and the seashore, from the depths of the abyss to the splash zone, are inhabited by a wide variety of living creatures. They differ very greatly and sometimes very misleadingly from those of the land : the holdfast of a seaweed looks like a root, though it is nothing of the sort ; and in spite of their appearance such creatures as the sea-lily and the flower-like anemone are not plants but animals.

So great is this difference that the life of the sea is full of interest ; nor is it lacking in beauty. It has, too, a special claim on our attention, for there is good reason to believe that the sea was the first home of life, and that all the land plants and animals—including ourselves—are descended from creatures of the sea. Human blood has indeed certain affinities with brine.

### Food-chains

In the sea, as on land, the plants, under the action of the light and by means of the green

**Plate 18** PLANTS OF SAND DUNES

1. Sea-rocket, *Cakile maritima* : 10 in.  2. Sea-holly, *Eryngium maritimum* : 12 in.  3. Prickly saltwort, *Salsola kali* : 18 in.
4. Sea-spurge, *Euphorbia paralias* : 12 in.  5. Sand-sedge, *Carex arenaria* : 9 in.  6. Marram grass, *Ammophila arenaria* : 3 ft.  7. Sand couch grass, *Agropyron junceiforme* : 2 ft.

substance chlorophyll, can absorb material from their surroundings and use it to build up their bodies. The animals, having no such power, have to live on the bodies of the plants or of other animals, their own waste products helping to provide some of the material which the plants absorb. There is thus a series of food-chains, some with endless complications, by which the living creatures can subsist on one another.

## PARASITISM AND SYMBIOSIS

Living creatures can also be related in other ways. One may be *parasitic* upon another, living upon or even inside its body without conferring any benefit upon it, and perhaps even preying upon it. (The term, appropriately enough, comes from Greek words which might be translated ' getting food on the side '.)

Two creatures may, however, be associated quite harmlessly because they live on the same sort of food ; this is called *commensalism* (Latin for ' a table together '). Their association may even be so close that they are practically merged into one body ; this joint life for mutual advantage is known as *symbiosis* (from the Greek for ' living together ').

## ATTACK AND DEFENCE

Animal life of sea and shore also resembles that of the land in that it is a matter of ' slay or be slain '. To get the food they need, and to avoid becoming food for others, the animals need means

of attack or defence and they have also to protect
themselves against their surroundings. Some are
heavily armed and armoured with powerful jaws
or pincers or waving tentacles, or with massive
shells covering their bodies. Some seek refuge in
sheltered places or utilize the discarded body
armour of other animals.

Some are camouflaged so as to escape their
enemies' notice, or are brightly coloured to warn
them off; some escape from attack, as though
under cover of a smoke-screen, by emitting a jet
of inky fluid. Some nonchalantly shed limbs
gripped by an enemy, or almost ' come to pieces '
to avoid its attack. Some bristle with threats or
allurements, warning their enemies off or enticing
their prey towards them until it is near enough to
grip. Some are firmly anchored to the rocks,
some drift passively wherever the water carries
them.

Examples of all these processes, including
parasitism, symbiosis and commensalism, will be
given in the appropriate sections.


## CLASSIFICATION

Like all other living creatures, the inhabitants of
the sea and seashore are classified by the Linnean
System devised in the eighteenth century by the
great Swedish botanist Karl von Linné (Linnaeus).
It is based on the idea of the *species*, a group of
creatures all of which are plainly ' the same sort
of thing ', differing only in minor details. Species
which in spite of their differences markedly

resemble one another are grouped to form a *genus*, and the genera are similarly grouped by their resemblances in families, sub-orders, orders, classes, phyla and kingdoms.

Plants and animals are technically known by their generic and specific names; only the commonest have ordinary English names. Though the former are unfamiliar and many of them are difficult, they form a guide to the creatures' relationships; they have, too, the advantage of being international. A few moreover are more attractive even than the common terms—compare, for example, jellyfish and *Aurelia*—and some of the common terms are misleading: a ' sea-cucumber ', for example, is not, as its name and appearance imply, a vegetable, but an animal.

# HABITATS

## PLANT AND ANIMAL COMMUNITIES

Naturalists use the term *habitat* for any region, on sea or land, which has its own typical plant and animal ' inhabitants ', and sea and seashore alike provide a wide variety of habitats, each with its own characteristic population.

Conditions near the surface of the sea naturally vary with the local climate, and they are very different from those somewhat below the surface, and still more from those in the ocean depths. Even more variable are conditions upon the shore ; these are more subject than those on land or in the ocean to continual fluctuations, arising from the

**Plate 19** PLANTS OF SALT-MARSH AND
TIDAL SHORE (pp. 102 and 105)

Many of the plants shown on other plates are found in salt-marshes.
1. Sea-aster, *Aster tripolium* : 2 ft. 2. Sea-milkwort, *Glaux
maritima* : 9 in. 3. Sea-purslane, *Halimione portulacoides* :
12 in. 4. Glasswort, *Salicornia stricta* : 6 in. 5. Seablite,
*Suaeda maritima* : 6 in. 6. Rice-grass, *Spartina townsendii* :
3 ft. 7. Eel-grass, *Zostera marina* : 9 in. or more.

periodic rise and fall of the tides. There may indeed be striking contrasts between the creatures which live in different parts of the same bay or even of the same rock-pool.

## IN THE SEA

Hitherto only tantalizing glimpses could be obtained of the creatures which live not on the shore but within the waters off our coasts. Now, thanks to the invention of skin-diving equipment and the aqualung, long periods can be spent beneath the waves. Thus it is possible to study the inhabitants of that strange submarine world which though it is, so to speak, on our doorstep is normally almost as completely hidden from our sight as the depths of the oceanic abyss or the landscapes of Venus or Mars.

## SHINGLE BEACHES

The pebbles of a shingle beach, almost devoid of water and often ground together by the waves, soon crush and destroy any living things ; so unfavourable are they to life that they can hardly be said to form a habitat. They are the nearest approach to a desert which our islands can show.

## SAND DUNES

The process by which the marram grass converts the sand dunes into a habitat where other plants and a few animals can live has already been discussed (p. 67). Studies made on the shores of Lake Michigan show that the grass and other hardy pioneers prepare a soil favourable to the growth of such bushes as junipers and aloes; these enrich the soil so that flowering plants and trees can take root in it.

## HIGH-WATER MARK ON THE SANDS

About high-water level the masses of seaweed and other oddments cast up by the tide form a limited habitat, providing sustenance for clouds of sand-hoppers and for beetles, flies and small worms.

## INTERTIDAL SANDS

The damp sand of the intertidal zone may seem almost lifeless, but this appearance is superficial. Hidden out of sight below its surface a variety of animals are either feeding or seeking food or are simply waiting for the tide to return.

Even if the surface is dried up by wind or sunshine, the underlying sand is still waterlogged, retaining the moisture between its particles by capillary action, the tendency of water to work its way into tiny crevices. Here, too, the temperature changes but little; and if a stream or a deluge of rain should drench the surface with fresh water this makes very little difference to the brine in the sands beneath, a liquid rich not only in plankton but in other organic material partly derived from decaying seaweed.

Some of the animals that live in the sand derive little nourishment from it until it is covered once more by the tide. Some pass it through their bodies, abstracting digestible material during the process. Some actively burrow through it in search of food.

The rising tide not merely replenishes the sand with brine but strews its surface with minute fragments of material which the animals can eat; other fragments of this material, as well as the plankton, are afloat in it. All the creatures in the sand can now find sustenance; some are *deposit feeders*, gathering their food from the material scattered on its surface, others are *suspension feeders* which drink in the brine and filter out its nourishment.

## MUD-FLATS

Where the sea flows feebly or is checked by the outflow of a river mouth, the material it deposits is not so much sand as finely grained mud. These mud-flats, though unattractive to the seaside visitor and perhaps even dangerously swampy, have their own characteristic population. They form not one habitat but several, grading into one another, for the water which flows through them varies from fresh through brackish to salt, the river plants and animals increasingly giving place to those of the sea. The animals which live on the surface of the mud also differ greatly from those buried in it.

## ROCKY SHORES

Unlike a beach, where the underlying sand below high tide level is always saturated with brine, conditions on a rocky shore vary greatly both from

**Plate 20** PLANTS OF CLIFFS AND ROCKS

1. Scurvy-grass, *Cochlearia officinalis* : 6 in. 2. Sea-spurrey, *Spergularia salina* : 12 in. 3. Samphire, *Crithmum maritimum* : 12 in. 4. Scots lovage, *Ligusticum scoticum* : 15 in. 5. Thrift or sea-pink, *Armeria maritima* : 9 in. 6. Rock sea-lavender, *Limonium binervosum* : 12 in. 7. Sea-plantain, *Plantago maritima* : 6 in. Some of these, especially 1, 2, 5 and 7, are common on other kinds of shore, especially salt-marsh, and 6 has a near relative in salt-marshes.

place to place and from time to time. Even beyond low tide level there is a *sublittoral zone* where the water is so shallow that the creatures which live in it are affected by changes in the light and heat of the sunshine.

Just above low tide level the shore is submerged almost throughout the day; beyond this the higher the shore is the longer it is uncovered by the sea—the part near high-water mark is submerged only for very short periods twice a day. Indeed, the very lowest part of the intertidal zone may be completely submerged, and the very highest part completely uncovered, for days on end, between one spring tide and the next. Finally, beyond the reach even of the spring tide at its highest, is the *splash zone*, which is intermittently drenched or spattered by the spray.

These varying conditions produce a number of habitats, grading into one another, on the same stretch of shore. Many marine animals could not tolerate the long periods of desiccation and exposure to sun and wind which prevail near high-water mark; others cannot endure too much sea. Most have limits which suit them but beyond which they perish; these are called their *zones* and their succession on a shore forms its *zonation*. To study and compare the different zonations on a few stretches of coast is very instructive.

The animals on the shore also have to adapt themselves to its changing conditions, which are produced not only by the rise and fall of the tide but by the weather and the season of the year. They have also to endure intermittent pounding by the waves, and changes in the salinity of the water in which they live. A small rock-pool, for example, may become even more salty than usual when its waters are evaporated by intense sunshine, and then suddenly be converted almost into fresh water by a sudden deluge of rain or the overflowing of an adjoining stream.

## WITHIN THE ROCKS

Strange as it may seem, several distinct types of animal can bore tunnels not only into the timber of piers or the hulls of ships but actually into the solid rock. Interesting to the biologist as these animals are, and important as they may be because of the damage they cause to harbour works and shipping, all that most of us are likely to see of them is the entrance to the holes they excavate.

## ROCK-POOLS

Of all the seashore habitats, the rock-pools are the most interesting and attractive. They are also the most varied, for they may be found almost anywhere and under the most diverse conditions in the intertidal zone. Some are tiny, some quite large. Some obviously teem with living creatures ; some seem almost devoid of life : the pebbles they contain, swirled by the waves, would crush almost anything that tried to live in them. Some are sheltered from wind or rain, others lie open to either or both. Some are rendered, by evaporation, a little more salty than the sea, others diluted by drainage from the shore—though in special

95

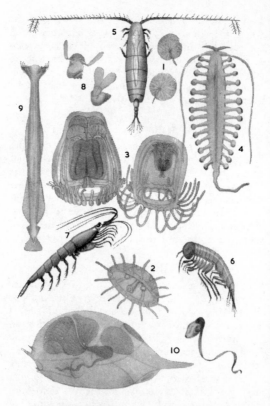

**Plate 21** ANIMALS OF THE PLANKTON

1. *Noctiluca scintillans* (p. 117): much enlarged. 2. *Obelia medusa*: ⅛ in. 3. *Turritopsis nutricula*: ⅛ in. 4. *Tomopteris helgolandica* (p. 147): 1 in. 5. *Calamus finmarchicus* (p. 190): ⅛ in. 6. *Themisto gracilipes*: much enlarged. 7. *Nyctiphanes couchi* (p. 199): to 1 in. 8. *Limacina retroversa* (p. 176): much enlarged. 9. Arrow-worm, *Sagitta setosa* (p. 100): ¾ in. 10. *Oikopleura dioica*: ⅛ in. (excluding tail).

circumstances this fresh water may not dilute the brine but simply form a layer on top of it and keep it from losing heat.

Not all the pool's inhabitants are in sight. Some are hidden among the seaweeds, below overhanging ledges, in crevices under the rocks, or beneath loose stones. Each of these minor habitats has its own special type of population.

To overturn a stone in a rock-pool, for example, may reveal numerous creatures very different from those that live elsewhere in the pool. They cannot survive anywhere except under their stone, nor could the creatures on the upper surface of the stone survive if it were overturned on top of them.

FOR THIS REASON ANY STONE WHICH IS MOVED OR OVERTURNED SHOULD BE REPLACED AS QUICKLY AS POSSIBLE IN ITS FORMER POSITION AND RIGHT SIDE UP.

# THE PLANKTON

### THE DRIFTING LIFE OF THE SEA

If a finely meshed net is drawn through the sea it gradually collects a variety of living creatures together with a greenish-brown scum. The microscope shows that this scum largely consists of an even wider variety of much smaller creatures, including many which, in spite of their small size, have a very complicated structure.

Of the innumerable inhabitants of the sea some, the *benthos*, are attached to its floor or buried in the mud ; others, the *nekton*, can swim freely in the water. Those which simply drift in it and are carried about by its movements form the *plankton*.

The plankton includes both plants and animals ; and here, as elsewhere, the plants build up their bodies from the materials around them under the action of light. Most of them, therefore, live near enough to the surface for the sunshine to reach them ; though bacteria, which form plant life of a sort, have been found even in mud several miles down. They form food for the animals, whether for the tiny animals in the plankton or for larger creatures ; some of the whales live on the plankton itself.

After death the bodies of the creatures which live near the surface sink into the depths, thus providing food for the animals that live far below, and which are not, like the plants, dependent on the daylight. Whereas the vegetable life of the ocean is chiefly found near the surface, certain animals can thrive even in the abyss, subsisting partly on the dead bodies that drift slowly down to them.

These deep-living animals nevertheless depend, as do all marine animals, on the vegetation of the sea, most of which lives in the plankton. Invisible to sight except as a slight discoloration of the sea water, and otherwise perceptible only by the bitter taste they help to impart to it, the microscopic plants of the plankton have well been called the ' pastures of the sea '—and very lush pastures they are. It has even been suggested that they might be cultivated as a direct source of human food.

The recurring seasons have as great an effect on the life of the sea as they have on that of the land. In the dark days of winter the plants in the plankton, deprived of much of the light they need, rapidly decrease in number, and the animals in the plankton, deprived of the plants on which they feed and preyed on by the larger animals, show a corresponding decrease. Meanwhile, however, the decaying bodies of plants and animals alike replenish in the water the supply of such non-living materials as phosphates which all living creatures need; it is almost as if the sea were being manured ready for the spring.

When the brighter sunshine of spring returns, this material is ready for the plants in the plankton to absorb. This enables the plants to proliferate —within a fortnight they may increase ten thousandfold!—and this abundance of plant food enables the animals also to proliferate. Thus occurs what is called the *spring outburst* of marine life. Soon, however, it is checked; the plants, having absorbed almost all the material around them, are unable to increase further, and most of them are eaten by the animals, who then begin to perish for lack of food.

Many of the creatures die off, and the material from their decaying bodies sinks into the depths, too low for the plants near the surface to make use of it. During the autumn, however, the gales churn the seas and bring this material to the surface. Here the plants at once absorb it; again they proliferate, and again the food they provide enables the animals to proliferate. Though it is less productive than that of the spring, this *autumn outburst* of sea life supplies enough material to enable the plankton to survive during the winter.

## PLANTS OF THE PLANKTON

The plants of the plankton are of three main types, all extremely small and floating freely in the water: the *diatoms*, encased in exquisitely sculptured cell walls of the flinty material silica; the *dinoflagellates*, with two whip-like lashes by means of which they move about; and the plant members of the even more minute community of organisms called collectively the *nannoplankton*.

## ANIMALS OF THE PLANKTON

The animals of the plankton are more diverse than the plants. Some, most of them very small, remain in it throughout their life. The *copepods* ('oar feet'), so plentiful that they form the chief food of the herring, resemble tiny shrimps, about a fifth of an inch long; the *krill*, upon which some of the whales largely subsist, are also shrimp-like but may be an inch or so long. The *arrow-worms*, which are even larger, up to three inches long, have powerful jaws enabling them to prey on other animals: that illustrated (Plate 21, 9) is *Sagitta setosa*. There are also *salps* something like sea-squirts (*see* p. 125), *sea-butterflies* with paper-thin shells, and countless microscopic animals whose silica or calcareous shells help to form the ooze on the sea-floor.

Some animals, though fairly large, are unable to swim and so form part of the plankton. The air-filled floats of the Portuguese men-o'-war, which the wind blows across the sea like a sail, may be six inches across, and their tentacles may be as much as sixty feet long. These jellyfish are sometimes washed up on the British beaches, and their tentacles can inflict very painful stings on anyone rash enough to touch them.

The plankton also contains the eggs or spawn or immature forms of animals which in later life fasten themselves to the rocks, burrow into the sand or swim freely through the water. Many of them are surprisingly different from their adult forms. Some of the larvae found in the plankton are shown on Plate **33**.

A magnified illustration of some of the animals in the plankton is given on Plate **21**.

## PLANTS OF THE SEASHORE

Conditions close to the sea encourage the growth of a vegetation differing somewhat from that of regions inland. Some of the plants thrive in a salt-laden soil, others in a soil lacking in water, and others in conditions which ordinary plants would soon find fatal.

Marram grass, *Ammophila arenaria* (Plate **18**, *6*),

for example, can not only live on the barren sand dunes but can survive even when buried by the drifting sand ; it simply grows new shoots above the newly formed surface and sends new runners down below. Together with sand couch grass, *Agropyron junceiforme* (Plate **18**, *7*), and sand-sedge, *Carex arenaria* (Plate **18**, *5*), it is of special importance in the stabilization of dunes. Other plants which can grow on the sand include sea-beet, *Beta maritima* (Plate **17**, *6*), and prickly saltwort, *Salsola kali* (Plate **18**, *3*). Orache, *Atriplex patula* (Plate **17**, *7*), like several similar members of the genus, is widely distributed on many kinds of shore ; it is also found inland.

Some of the plants found on shingle and sandy foreshores are shown on Plate **17**, and some of those found on sand dunes on Plate **18** ; naturally there is some overlapping between the two types of plant. Sea-campion, *Silene maritima* (Plate **17**, *2*), and sea-beet may also occur on cliffs.

On pebbles continually rolled about by the waves very little can survive. When parts of a shingle beach become stable, however, odd patches of drifted soil and humus (vegetable mould) collect on its surface, while dew and rain accumulate between the pebbles to give a scanty supply of fresh water. A few sturdy plants take root on these patches ; among them is the seablite, *Suæda maritima* (Plate **19**, *5*), which if covered by a movement of the pebbles will survive by growing new roots around its buried stems.

In contrast with these, the salt-marshes have a varied plant population. Here the glasswort,

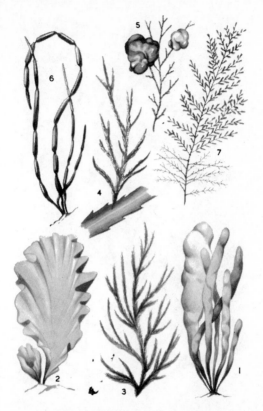

**Plate 22** GREEN AND BROWN SEAWEEDS (pp. 106–108)
1. *Enteromorpha intestinalis* : to 18 in.  2. Sea-lettuce, *Ulva lactuca* : 6 in.  3. *Cladophora rupestris* : to 6 in.  4. *Ectocarpus confervoides* : to 6 in. or more.  5. *Leathesia difformis* : 12 in.
6. *Scytosiphon lomentarius* : 16 in.  7. *Desmarestia aculeata* : to 3 ft., summer form above, winter form below.

**Plate 23**  SEA-WRACKS (pp. 108 and 111)

1. Channelled wrack, *Pelvetia canaliculata* : to 6 in.  2. Flat wrack, *Fucus spiralis* : to 12 in.  3. Bladder wrack, *Fucus vesiculosus* : to 3 ft.  3a. *Elachista fucicola* on *Fucus* : 1 in.  4. Knotted wrack, *Ascophyllum nodosum* : to 6 ft.  4a. *Polysiphonia lanosa* (red seaweed) : to 4 in.  5. Serrated wrack, *Fucus serratus* : to 6 ft.  6. Pod-weed, *Halidrys siliquosa* : to 4 ft.

*Salicornia stricta*, and rice-grass, *Spartina towns-endii* (Plate **19**, *4*, *6*), [1] act on the mud much as the marram grass does on sand. These are the earliest plants to colonize the mud, and they stabilize it so that other plants can grow on it, such as the sea-aster, *Aster tripolium*, sea-milkwort, *Glaux maritima*, and sea-purslane, *Halimione portulacoides* (Plate **19**, *1*, *2*, *3*), in the lower reaches of the flat and the scurvy-grass, *Cochlearia officinalis*, sea-spurrey, *Spergularia salina*, and sea-plantain, *Plantago maritima* (Plate **20**, *1*, *2*, *7*), in its middle and upper reaches. The sea-lavender, *Limonium vulgare*, also grows on the marshes, and the eel-grass, *Zostera marina* (Plate **19**, *7*), grows on muddy shores even beyond the low-water mark.

Many of these salt-marsh plants, notably the sea-aster, sea-milkwort, sea-purslane and sea-lavender, also grow on rocky shores; here too may be found the samphire, *Crithmum maritimum*, the Scots lovage, *Ligusticum scoticum*, the rock sea-lavender, *Limonium binervosum*, and thrift, *Armeria maritima* (Plate **20**, *3*, *4*, *6*, *5*). These may be found not only on the rocks near the shore but on the ledges and projections of the cliff face, and even in the joints of a sea-wall.

They also grow on the cliff top, along with such land plants as the gorse and heath. In these exposed positions few trees can flourish, and their

---

[1] The rice-grass, which has appeared only in fairly recent times, is apparently a cross between that long-established marsh plant the cord grass and some other grass of North American origin, probably brought quite accidentally across the Atlantic.

trunks, instead of being erect, may be blown obliquely by the prevailing winds from the sea.

# SEAWEEDS AND LICHENS

## SEAWEEDS

Unlike the land plants, the seaweeds (*algæ*) have no flowers, no clearly marked stems or leaves and, in spite of appearances, no roots : what looks like a seaweed's root is really its *holdfast*, which does not absorb food but simply attaches the plant firmly to a stone or rock.

Yet the seaweeds are true plants, and like other plants they contain chlorophyll ; in many of them, however, its green colour is obscured by other substances. There are thus not only green but also brown and red seaweeds, though these colours may be difficult to distinguish and all seaweeds turn white when they are dead. There are also blue-green seaweeds (Cyanophyceae), but these are too small to study ; they form part of the black material which accumulates on many shores at high-water mark.

## Green seaweeds

The green seaweeds (Chlorophyceæ) are chiefly found on the upper shore, where there may be rivulets and pools of fresh water. The tubular fronds of *Enteromorpha intestinalis* (Plate **22**, *1*) are bright green, and the gas they contain makes them swell out in fresh water, but when dry they deflate and flatten and turn white. The thin green fronds of the sea-lettuce or green laver, *Ulva lactuca*

(Plate **22**, *2*), do not grow so high up the shore ; this plant is sometimes collected for food. The dark green tufts which abound in the shady parts of the rocks are those of *Cladophora rupestris* (Plate **22**, *3*) ; the tufts of *Bryopsis plumosa* are more delicate and feathery, and grow in the rock-pools.

## Brown seaweeds

The brown seaweeds (Phæophyceæ), whose colours range from brown to olive-green, form the various sea-wracks which cover so much of the shore. They show a clear zonation, some of them being limited to belts at fairly definite heights along the shore. Their fronds branch, and many of them expand into small bladders which keep them afloat in the sea ; this enables them to get more sunshine than would otherwise be possible. So buoyant are some of the wracks that they may lift clear of the sea-floor the stone to which they are attached ; then seaweed and stone together are carried inshore by the rising tide, possibly beyond the zone in which the seaweed can live.

The brown seaweeds shown on Plate **22** are smaller species. *Ectocarpus confervoides* (Plate **22**, *4*) is a common member of a large genus of fluffy brown seaweeds which often grow on larger seaweeds. The illustration shows its appearance when out of the water ; in water it spreads into a cloud of filaments so fine as to be almost indistinguishable. *Leathesia difformis* (Plate **22**, *5*) is found on other seaweeds or on rocks, and is very common in summer ; it is found on coralline (*see* p. 114). *Scytosiphon lomentarius* (Plate **22**, *6*) is also found on other seaweeds or on rocks, and is also common. *Desmarestia aculeata* (Plate **22**, *7*) is found near low-water mark on rocky shores; it is a perennial and the delicate branching filaments which clothe it in summer die off to leave a tough, coarse, serrated plant in winter. In the illustration the summer form is shown above and the winter form below.

The channelled wrack, *Pelvetia canaliculata* (Plate **23**, *1*), which can tolerate much exposure and desiccation, and indeed dies if submerged for too long, occupies the highest zone of the brown seaweeds, near the high-water mark of spring tides or even in the splash zone. The groove from which it is named, along one side of its fronds, helps it to retain moisture. When dry the fronds turn black and seem to shrivel up, but when during the high spring tides they absorb water they regain their normal olive-green colour.

Somewhat lower down the shore comes the flat wrack, *Fucus spiralis* (Plate **23**, *2*). This has no bladders, but the ends of its fronds often have a swollen appearance. It too darkens and twists together when dry, but its fronds then lack the shrivelled appearance of the channelled wrack.

Along the middle part of the shore two brown seaweeds are recognizable by the air bladders on their fronds. Those on the bladder wrack, *Fucus vesiculosus* (Plate **23**, *3*), are paired, one each side of the midrib, whereas those on the leathery

**Plate 24**  TANGLES AND DULSE (pp. 111–112)

1. Bootlace weed, *Chorda filum :* to 20 ft.  2. Oar-weed, *Laminaria digitata :* to 6 ft.  3. *Laminaria saccharina :* to 8 ft. 4. Thong weed, *Himanthalia elongata:* to 6 ft. or more.  5. Dulse, *Rhodymenia palmata :* to 15 in.  6. *Dilsea carnosa :* 12 in. (N.B. 5 and 6 are red seaweeds.)

**Plate 25**  RED SEAWEEDS (pp. 112–113)

1. *Furcellaria fastigiata* : to 10 in.  2. *Rhodomela subfusca* : to
10 in.  3. Pepper-dulse, *Laurencia pinnatifida* : to 12 in.  4.
*Ptilota plumosa* :  to 19 in.  5. *Ceramium rubrum* : to 12 in.
6. Carragheen, *Chondrus crispus* : 6 in.  7. *Gigartina stellata* :
to 8 in.  8. *Lomentaria articulata* : to 8 in.

knotted wrack, *Ascophyllum nodosum* (Plate **23**, *4*), occur singly and are wider than the fronds themselves. These two seaweeds do not normally occur together; the bladder wrack, found not only in sheltered but in exposed places, can endure more buffeting by the waves than the knotted wrack, which prefers quieter conditions and is mostly found on reefs, though it also grows on boulders in sheltered waters. *Elachista fucicola*, a brown plant which grows on seaweeds, is shown on the bladder wrack (Plate **23**, *3a*). Similar plants occur on this and other seaweeds. *Polysiphonia lanosa* (Plate **23**, *4a*) is a red seaweed—almost always found with the knotted wrack on which it lives as a parasite, penetrating the tissues of the host with little root-like structures.

The seaweed which makes the rocks near low tide level so slippery is the serrated wrack, *Fucus serratus* (Plate **23**, *5*), named from the irregular edges of its fronds. Pod-weed, *Halidrys siliquosa* (Plate **23**, *6*), is a similar type of seaweed common in deep pools or below low-water mark.

Some seaweeds which grow at and beyond low water level are often washed higher up the shore. They are called tangle weeds or oar-weed; under the name of kelp they have been collected and burned as a source of alkalis or iodine. The first to be exposed at low tide is oar-weed, *Laminaria digitata* (Plate **24**, *2*); its stalk is smooth, hard and stiff, and its fronds are broad and split into several 'fingers'. *Laminaria saccharina* (Plate **24**, *3*), so called because it contains a sugar, forms long flat fronds, which may be up to eight feet in length and a foot wide.

Thong weed, *Himanthalia elongata* (Plate **24**, *4*), gets its name from its appearance, and grows from a toadstool-like button, which may be found even when the seaweed itself is missing. Even more thong-like is the bootlace weed, *Chorda filum* (Plate **24**, *1*), whose fronds, which may be ten feet long, grow not from a ' button ' but from a holdfast attached to stones or shells.

## Red seaweeds

The red seaweeds (Rhodophyceæ), many of which grow near the low tide level, are not so familiar as the brown. One of the most common is the dulse, *Rhodymenia palmata* (Plate **24**, *5*), which is often found attached to the stalks of *Laminaria* ; it has long been used as a food in western Scotland and Ireland. *Dilsea carnosa* (Plate **24**, *6*) has been confused with dulse, but though edible is less frequently used. The pink colour of these algæ comes out in fresh water, and in classical times may have served as a cosmetic.

The plants shown on Plate **25** are small, branching species with narrower fronds than the above. *Furcellaria fastigiata* (Plate **25**, *1*) is found usually in pools on rocky shores. *Rhodomela subfusca* (Plate **25**, *2*) forms bushy tufts on rocks and smaller stones or shells. Pepper-dulse, *Laurencia pinnatifida* (Plate **25**, *3*), may be found at almost any level on rocky shores. The colour varies from the typical red to shades of greenish yellow, according to the amount of sunlight it receives, and the growth form also varies somewhat in relation to tidal level. *Ptilota plumosa* (Plate **25**, *4*) is a common growth on stems of oar-weed.

*Ceramium rubrum* (Plate **25**, *5*) is one of many filamentous species, commonly attached to other seaweeds or to stones. It is variable in form but can be recognized by the tips of the branches which appear through a lens like little forceps.

Carragheen, also called Irish moss, *Chondrus crispus* (Plate **25**, *6*), serves as a food and is used in jellies and similar commodities ; during the Second World War it provided a valuable medium for bacteriological work. It varies greatly in shape and colour and is so abundant that on exposed shores it sometimes replaces the brown seaweeds. *Gigartina stellata* (Plate **25**, *7*) is equally common and may be found growing with the carragheen. The smaller *Lomentaria articulata* (Plate **25**, *8*) grows on rocks, and on other seaweeds near low water.

Some of the red seaweeds give a special beauty to the rock-pools. The purple laver, *Porphyra umbilicalis* (Plate **26**, *1*), grows abundantly on rocky shores and sometimes spreads on to drifted sand ; its thin 'leaves', divided into lobes, provide the food known in Wales as laverbread.

Some of the other red seaweeds have 'leaves' somewhat resembling those of land plants ; one of the most attractive is *Delesseria sanguinea* (Plate **26**, *2*), which occurs in deep pools and other shady places. The fronds of *Phycodrys rubens* resemble oak leaves, and are usually attached to the stalks of *Laminaria*.

Coral-weed, also called coralline, *Corallina officinalis* (Plate **26**, *3*), abundant in the rock-pools, is a red seaweed which is hardened, and almost given a ' skeleton ', by lime, but this is sufficiently jointed to allow flexibility ; its colour varies with exposure to light, and indeed the plant may be bleached to whiteness. *Lithophyllum incrustans* (Plate **26**, *4*) is another calcareous (limy) seaweed which forms a thin encrustation, purple-pink to white or grey, on rock and sometimes even on other seaweeds.

## SEAWEED REPRODUCTION

The seaweeds reproduce by a method suggestive rather of an animal than a plant. From the swollen tips of some of the fronds emerge countless male and female cells, which unite to form tiny spores ; these become part of the plankton. Many are eaten, many washed out to sea or on to sand or muddy shores where they cannot live, but some find their way to a suitable habitat.

## THE ' JUNGLES OF THE SHORE '

Checking the movements of the water, the floating strands of some of the seaweeds produce a minor habitat in which certain plants and animals can flourish. Along the fronds of the knotted wrack grow tufts of small red seaweeds, and the holdfasts of the larger seaweeds provide a home for an incredible number of microscopic creatures —there may be tens, or even hundreds, of thousands to a square yard of rock! Just as the plankton forms the ' pastures of the sea ', the seaweeds, providing sheltered conditions for a wealth of animal life, might equally be called the ' jungles of the shore '.

## LICHENS

The lichens (sometimes pronounced as spelled, sometimes as ' lykens ') form an excellent example of symbiosis, being composed of a fungus and an algae. Their association makes them hardy enough to live in exacting habitats ; high-water mark may be shown on the rocks by an horizontal black line of the lichens *Verrucaria maura* mingled with the blue-green seaweeds.

Of others at this high level the most common is *Xanthoria parietina* (Plate **26**, *7*), usually orange-coloured but sometimes green in the shade. The green-grey *Ramalina* (Plate **26**, *5*) may spread even above *Xanthoria*, and both may be intermingled with the grey, roughly granular *Lecanora* (Plate **26**, *8*).

*Lichina pygmæa* (Plate **26**, *6*) occurs in patches on the rocks an inch or two across, and might be mistaken for a brown seaweed. *Lichina confinis* also resembles a tiny seaweed and may be found above high-water mark, even towards the upper limit of the splash zone.

**Plate 26** LAVER, CORALLINES AND LICHENS
(pp. 113–115)

1. Purple laver, *Porphyra umbilicalis* : to 10 in. 2. *Delesseria sanguinea* : to 8 in. 3. Coralline, *Corallina officinalis* : to 6 in. 4. *Lithophyllum incrustans* : variable patches. 5. *Ramalina* : 1½ in. 6. *Lichina pygmaea* : to 1 in. 7. *Xanthoria parietina* : 4 in. across. 8. *Lecanora* : variable patches.

# SPONGES, SEA-MATS, ETC.

The simplest animals are the *Protozoa*, whose bodies consist only of one solitary cell, a microscopic blob of living matter. Abundant though they are, they are too small for most of us to notice. One, however, has a shell visible as a tiny brown ball about a twelfth of an inch in diameter, attached to seaweed holdfasts or stones : this is *Gromia oviformis*, a shore protozoan.

Many protozoans live in the plankton, along with those tiny plants the flagellates. One of the latter, *Noctiluca scintillans* (Plate **21**, *1*), feeds like an animal and so is included here ; it is best known by its effects, for it is mainly responsible for night-time phosphorescence on the surface of the sea.

## MANY-CELLED ANIMALS

The vast majority of living creatures consist of multitudinous cells, specialized to carry out various functions but all co-operating to form one plant or animal body. Every creature, however, no matter how complex or numerous its cells, began life as one cell and grew to maturity through a process of repeated subdivision.

## Sponges

Among the simplest many-celled animals are the sponges, the *Porifera* (' cavity bearers '), whose body walls have a number of openings leading into channels which extend throughout the body. These channels are lined with cells provided with flagellae, moving whip-like threads which draw a continuous current of water into a central chamber; its food particles having been absorbed, the water is then expelled through one or more of the larger openings.

The body wall is strengthened by a horny material, spongin, or by small spicules of a hard limy or flinty substance. A sponge may be colourful, and its shape and size vary with the conditions in which it lives. Eggs form in the wall and mostly develop into tiny larvæ which emerge and soon settle down on a suitable surface to grow into new sponges; some sponges also reproduce by forming and liberating buds.

Many sponges, apart from producing currents in the water around them, give no signs of life, and seem so inert that they were once thought to be not animals but plants. They simply consist of a mass of soft ' spongy ' material encrusting the surface of the rock.

The most common of these, known from its appearance as the breadcrumb sponge, *Halichondria panicea* (Plate **28**, *6*), forms a yellowish, greenish, greyish or orange encrustation on rocks and other surfaces under water; except for the openings of its pores, its surface is smooth. The surface of the blood-red sponge, *Hymeniacidon perleve* (Plate **28**, *5*), is roughened by a number of irregular grooves as well as by its pores; it may be found in crevices in the rock-pools and under overhanging ledges.

The purse sponges project something after the

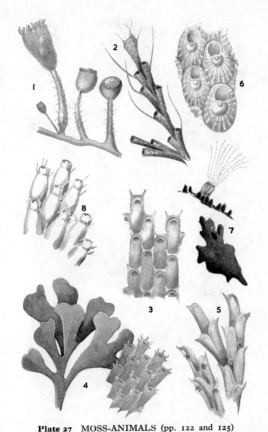

**Plate 27** MOSS-ANIMALS (pp. 122 and 125)

1. *Pedicellina cernua*: ½ in. 2. *Crisia eburnea*: to 1 in. 3. Sea-mat, *Membranipora membranacea*: much enlarged. 4. Horn wrack, *Flustra foliacea*: left, ½ natural size, right, much enlarged. 5. *Bugula plumosa*: much enlarged. 6. *Umbonula verrucosa*: much enlarged. 7. *Alcyonidium hirsutum*: above, much enlarged, below, ½ natural size. 8. *Flustrella hispida*: much enlarged.

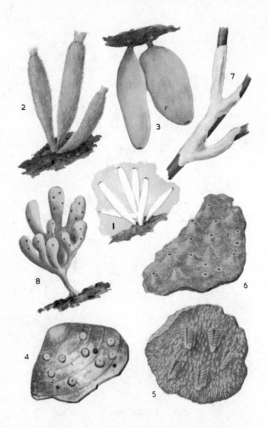

**Plate 28** SPONGES

1. *Leucosolenia botryoides* : ¼–½ in. 2. *Sycon ciliatum* : to 1½ in.
3. Purse sponge, *Grantia compressa* : 2 in. 4. Boring sponge,
*Cliona celata*: projecting ½ in. 5. Blood-red sponge, *Hymeniacidon
perleve* : extensive. 6. Breadcrumb sponge, *Halichondria
panicea* : extensive. 7. Slime sponge, *Halisarca dujardini* :
extensive, thin. 8. Mermaid's gloves, *Haliclona oculata* : to
12 in.

style of vases; an example is the mermaid's gloves, *Haliclona oculata* (Plate **28**, *8*), which has tiny openings on the sides of its branches and stands erect on the rocks or seaweed. *Leucosolenia botryoides* (Plate **28**, *1*) is branched and has been compared to a tiny bunch of bananas; it is commonly found on seaweeds. *Sycon ciliatum* (Plate **28**, *2*) gets its name from its bristling hair-like spicules. The purse sponge itself, *Grantia compressa* (Plate **28**, *3*), hangs down from the lower surface of boulders and projecting rocks or may be attached to the red seaweeds.

The boring sponges, *Cliona celata* (Plate **28**, *4*), are able to excavate holes in shells, and even in limestone rocks, by means of the acid their bodies produce and their flinty spicules. They live inside these holes like small yellow spongy lumps, but when under water they sometimes protrude slightly. An old oyster or scallop shell lying on the beach may be dotted with their holes, and the boring sponges have done much harm on the oyster-beds.

The slime sponge, *Halisarca dujardini* (Plate **28**, *7*), resembles the other sponges only in having the usual openings. It has neither spongin nor limy or flinty spicules, and simply forms a thin jelly-like sheet on the surface, for example, of the red seaweed.

## Sea-mats

Patches of a network resembling lace may be found in many places on the surfaces of the stones and rocks and also of the sea-shells and crabs and fronds of seaweed. These sea-mats are one form of the creatures known as *Bryozoa* (' moss-animals ') or *Polyzoa* (' many animals ').

The Bryozoa form dense colonies, each individual in the colony having its own little chamber of limy or horny material. A lens shows that each has a mouth surrounded by a circle of tentacles ; on these are a number of cilia, whose movements produce currents of water which carry particles of food into the mouth. The animal can retire into its ' cell ' or project from its opening, which in some kinds is surrounded by teeth. Among these openings may be some shaped rather like a beak ; these can open and close sharply, keeping other creatures from forming a crust over the colony and smothering it ; some of the animals also keep the whole colony clear of mud particles. The eggs of the Bryozoa hatch into larvæ, the *cyphonautes* (Plate **33**, *4*), which after floating about as part of the plankton settle down and divide into a new colony by budding.

The sea-mat, *Membranipora membranacea* (Plate **27**, *3*), is the type of encrusting Bryozoa most frequently seen ; it spreads like lace over the oar-weeds. Another, *Alcyonidium hirsutum* (Plate **27**, *7*), a thick greenish coating of gelatinous material often found on seaweeds, might be mistaken for a sponge : a related type, *Alcyonidium gelatinosum*, forms larger colonies which often grow erect with blunt projections. Another, *Flustrella hispida* (Plate **27**, *8*), forms dark reddish-brown colonies on the lower parts of the stems of some of the seaweeds ; its spines give the

**Plate 29** SEA-FIRS (pp. 130, 133 and 134)

1. Oaten-pipes hydroid, *Tubularia indivisa* : to 4 in. or more.
2. *Coryne pusilla* : 4 in. 3. *Clava squamata* : to 1 in.
4. *Hydractinia echinata* : ⅛ in. 5. *Clytia johnstoni* : ⅛ in.
6. *Obelia geniculata* : to 3 in. 7. *Laomedea flexuosa* : 1 in.
8. Sea-oak, *Dynamena pumila* : to 1½ in. These figures depict
a few members of large colonies. Sizes refer to the height of the
whole colony.

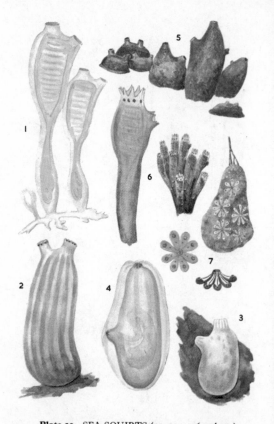

**Plate 30** SEA-SQUIRTS (pp. 125, 126 and 129)

1. *Clavelina lepadiformis* : 1–2 in. high. 2. Tube sea-squirt,
*Ciona intestinalis* : 2 in. 3. Rough sea-squirt, *Ascidiella scabra* :
1½ in. 4. *Ascidia mentula* : 1 in. 5. Gooseberry sea-squirt,
*Dendrodoa grossularia* : ¼–½ in. 6. *Morchellium argus* : 1½ in.
(individual enlarged on left). 7. Star sea-squirt or golden star,
*Botryllus schlosseri* : 1 in. (and two enlarged 'stars').

whole colony a rough 'hairy' appearance. *Umbonula verrucosa* (Plate **27**, *6*) forms rose-red patches, up to two inches across, on stones and rocks and among the holdfasts of *Laminaria*, the brown seaweeds.

There are also tufted or branching Bryozoa. *Crisia eburnea* (Plate **27**, *2*) forms white tufts, up to an inch in length, on the red seaweed and on stones. The horn wrack, *Flustra foliacea* (Plate **27**, *4*), lives normally below low-water mark, but may be washed up on the shore after storms; its broad flattened branches might be mistaken for fronds of seaweed until closer examination shows its network arrangement. The delicate brownish branching colonies of *Bugula plumosa* (Plate **27**, *5*) are mostly attached to the rocks.

*Pedicellina cernua* (Plate **27**, *1*), another colonial animal whose members form tiny open-mouthed 'bells' on stalks about a fifth of an inch long, has a superficial resemblance to the Bryozoa. Its structure, however, is so different that it is grouped in a separate phylum, the *Entoprocta*.

## SEA-SQUIRTS

Animals of very different types which live in similar circumstances and on similar foods may come to resemble one another, so that the sea-squirts (tunicates or ascidians) might easily be mistaken for sponges. They consist of translucent or jelly-like material, sometimes a few inches long, adhering to the rocks, and like the sponges they may form colonies; they live, moreover, by passing currents of sea water through their bodies and absorbing the edible material they carry. In the compound kinds one aperture for discharging water serves several individuals.

The tunicates are, however, quite different from the sponges. Their soft bodies are covered with a tough leathery or gelatinous ' tunic ' or ' test ' —hence the name. A sea-squirt of a solitary type is usually attached to the rock by its base or side, and has two openings in its tunic ; these may be lengthened into siphons, one of which draws in water while the other expels it, meanwhile passing it through a fine mesh which entraps the plankton. If, however, the sea-squirt is gently pressed it will at once justify its name by emitting a jet of water from both siphons and contracting into a small blob of jelly ; this enables it to be distinguished from the sponges, which simply yield passively to the pressure.

The tube sea-squirt, *Ciona intestinalis* (Plate **30**, *2*), a solitary form, lives under stones or in crevices, and is also common on piers, buoys, and the hulls of ships. The rough sea-squirt, *Ascidiella scabra* (Plate **30**, *3*), is attached to stones or weeds by one of its sides, though another related type, *Ascidiella aspersa*, found only on the southern and western coasts, is attached by its base. *Ascidia mentula* (Plate **30**, *4*) is also found on the southern and western coasts, but not in Scotland or on the eastern coasts ; it may be greenish or a translucent red.

The gooseberry sea-squirt, *Dendrodoa grossularia* (Plate **30**, *5*), one of the commonest of the tunicates,

**Plate 31**   JELLYFISH AND COMB-JELLY
(pp. 134, 135 and 137)

1. Bell jellyfish, *Haliclystus auricula* : ⅓ in. high. 2. Moon jelly,
*Aurelia aurita* : to 8 in. across. 3. 'Lion's mane', *Cyanea
capillata* : to 24 in. 4. Compass jellyfish, *Chrysaora hyoscella* :
to 12 in. across. 5. *Rhizostoma octopus* : to 2 ft. across. 6. Sea-
gooseberry, *Pleurobrachia pileus* : ⅝–¾ in. long.

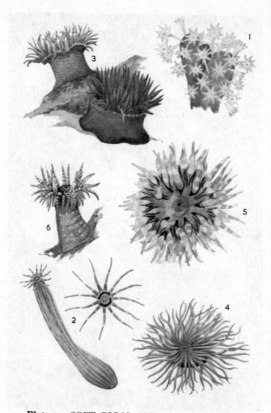

**Plate 32** SOFT CORAL AND SEA-ANEMONES
(pp. 138, 139 and 141)

1. Dead men's fingers or soft coral, *Alcyonium digitatum* : colonies
to 8 in. 2. *Peachia hastata* : 5 in. 3. Beadlet anemone, *Actinia
equina* : 1½ in. high, 2½ in. across. 4. Snake-locks or opelet
anemone, *Anemonia sulcata* : 4 in. (including tentacles). 5. Dahlia
anemone, *Tealia felina* : 2 in. across. 6. Wartlet or gem anemone,
*Bunodactis verrucosa* : 1 in. high, ⅜ in. across.

might be classed either as solitary or colonial, as its individuals may be attached to one another. They are quite small, up to about half an inch high, and they vary in shape, the taller ones being found where several cluster together ; they may be made more difficult to distinguish by a covering of mud. *Clavelina lepadiformis* (Plate **30**, *1*) is soft and transparent and lives on rocky shores at low-water mark ; its individuals, one to two inches high, are connected by a branching ' stolon ' into which they die down during the winter. In *Morchellium argus* (Plate **30**, *6*) the individuals are more closely attached, forming colonies abundant under stones or overhanging rocks.

Among the compound tunicates the golden star, also called the star sea-squirt, *Botryllus schlosseri* (Plate **30**, *7*), gets its name because of the pattern it forms, a number of ' petals ' grouped round its central outlet, which belongs to the whole colony. In *Botrylloides leachi* the individuals form a pattern not of stars but of branching lines. These, and several others less common, form encrustations on the rocks and seaweeds.

Strange as it may seem, the biologists classify these lowly animals in the same phylum, the Chordata, as man ! The little free-swimming larvæ which hatch from tunicate eggs are tadpole-like in general shape and possess a rudimentary backbone and other features suggestive of those which appear at some stage of the development of the higher vertebrates. It is believed that all the vertebrates are evolved from creatures resembling tunicates which instead of settling down on the rocks retain a free-swimming form, and a rudimentary backbone, throughout their lives.


# SEA-FIRS, JELLYFISH, SEA-ANEMONES AND CORALS

## COELENTERATA

The Coelenterata (from the Greek for ' hollow stomachs ') include some of the most beautiful animals of the seashore. Their structure is comparatively simple, the body consisting of a jelly-like sac with a single opening, the mouth, surrounded by tentacles armed with stinging cells. Most of them feed on small animals, capturing and paralysing them with the cells on their tentacles and then drawing them into their mouths, through which their indigestible remains are afterwards rejected.

They occur in two different forms, which alternate during the life cycle of certain species. The *polyp* is attached to a solid surface by a basal disc. The *medusa* is a free-swimming form, the body expanding into a pulsating parachute-like float.

## Sea-firs

The sea-firs (hydroids) look so much like plants that they were formerly known as *zoophytes* (' plant-animals ') ; they might easily be mistaken for the Bryozoa (sea-mats). They form colonies which may be large enough to be visible to the

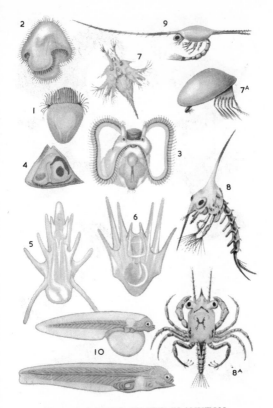

**Plate 33** LARVAE OF THE PLANKTON

1. Trochophore larva of *Phyllodoce* (p. 143). 2. Pilidium larva of a nemertine worm (p. 154). 3. Veliger larva of a mollusc (p. 164). 4. Cyphonautes larva of a bryozoan (p. 122). 5. Larva of a starfish, *Asterias* (p. 157). 6. Larva of a sea-urchin, *Echinus* (p. 160). 7 and 7a. Nauplius and cypris larvae of a barnacle, *Balanus* (p. 191). 8 and 8a. First and megalopa larvae of a crab, *Cancer* (p. 205). 9. Larva of a porcelain crab, *Porcellana* (p. 206). 10. Larvae of plaice, *Pleuronectes platessa* (p. 218).

**Plate 34** SEA-ANEMONES AND CUP CORAL
(pp. 141–142)

1. Plumose anemone, *Metridium senile* : 4 in. high. 2. Cave-dwelling anemone, *Sagartia troglodytes* : 1½ in. across. 3 and 3a. *Sagartia elegans* : 1½ in. across, 2½ in. high. 4. Daisy anemone, *Cereus pedunculatus* : 4 in. high. 5. Jewel anemone or globehorn, *Corynactis viridis* : ½ in. across. 6. Devonshire cup coral, *Caryophyllia smithii* : ¾ in. across.

unaided sight, though a lens is usually needed to study the individual polyps; this is best done in sea water, where the animals can expand. The individuals in the colony are connected by strands of living tissue, and the whole colony grows either by budding or by sexual reproduction. Medusae are budded off and these swim in the plankton; the fertilized eggs from these develop into new polyp colonies. The medusa is the adult animal and serves to distribute the eggs, which grow into the asexual bottom-living hydroids. In most shore hydroids the medusae never become free.

Many of the hydroids have a horny external skeleton, and in some types each of the polyps has a small cup into which it can withdraw. Other types have no such protection.

The oaten-pipes hydroid, *Tubularia indivisa* (Plate **29**, *1*), forms a mass of brown stems a few inches tall, mostly unbranched, on shells and stones along the edge of low tide; its reddish polyps are surrounded by two separate rings of tentacles. The branching stems of *Coryne pusilla* (Plate **29**, *2*) are somewhat smaller, and are marked by a number of rings; its widely separated tentacles end in knobs; it grows on rocks or weeds in sheltered places. The thread-like tentacles of *Clava squamata* (Plate **29**, *3*) are also widely separated and have no knobs; it grows in thick pinkish clusters about an inch tall on the knotted wrack. *Hydractinia echinata* (Plate **29**, *4*) forms patches of pink or brown on the shells occupied by the hermit crabs. None of these kinds has protective cups.

Some of the kinds that possess cups are attached to seaweed. The small, delicate *Clytia johnstoni* (Plate **29**, *5*) may appear when a stem of seaweed, usually one of the red weeds, is immersed in sea water. *Obelia geniculata* (Plate **29**, *6*) is more likely to be found on the oar-weeds and other brown seaweeds; its delicate stems grow in zigzag lines and when placed in sea water it may release its medusæ.

On rocky shores where the water is muddy *Laomedea flexuosa* (Plate **29**, *7*) may be found; it does not produce medusæ. The sea-oak, *Dynamena pumila* (Plate **29**, *8*), about an inch long, is the most common of all these animals, growing thickly on shells, stones and the stems of the brown seaweed. Relatives of this species grow so abundantly offshore on some parts of the coast that they are collected commercially, dried and dyed red or green for decorative purposes as ' sea-fern ', ' aqua-fern ', etc.

## Jellyfish

Though they may appear in the offshore waters or be left by the tide in the rock-pools, the jelly-fish (Scyphozoa) are creatures of the open sea; if stranded on the shore they not only die but dry up. In the sea they float parachute fashion; many are almost transparent with patches of blue, purple or orange. The reddish or purple brown-spotted *Pelagia noctiluca*, a few inches across, sometimes visible off the west and south-west coasts of England, is strongly phosphorescent, as is its adhesive slime.

Like many of the other hydroids the jellyfish alternate between the polyp and medusa stages, but here too the medusa is the adult animal. The eggs which they liberate into the sea become polyps, small, whitish, anemone-like animals with long-streaming tentacles usually attached to stones beyond low-water mark. They resemble the anemones, but in spring tiny saucer-like discs split off from the upper part of the body and grow into adult jellyfish.

Like the other coelenterates the jellyfish have tentacles surrounding their mouths, and the stinging cells of some species are so poisonous as to raise unpleasant weals on the skin. The brownish-yellow jellyfish *Cyanea capillata* (Plate **31**, *3*), known as the ' lion's mane ', is moderately common in British waters, where it is rarely more than two feet across. Equally dangerous is the smaller blue-violet *Cyanea lamarcki*, common in the North Sea and off southern coasts. The compass jellyfish, *Chrysaora hyoscella* (Plate **31**, *4*), which is also venomous and not uncommon, can be identified by its brown and white markings. In spite of the stinging cells the young of whiting and horse mackerel sometimes shelter unharmed beneath these animals.

The Portuguese man-o'-war, *Physalia physalis*, already mentioned as an animal of the plankton, is not one of the jellyfish but resembles them sufficiently to be included here. Its body is an oval bladder about six inches long, and is provided with a number of hanging tentacles. So poisonous is this animal that it is to be avoided even when

135

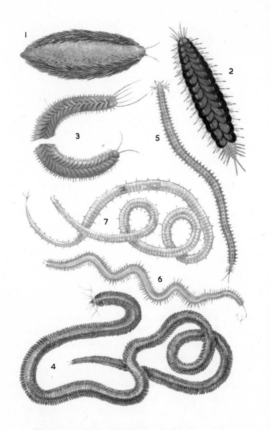

**Plate 35** SCALE-WORMS, ETC. (pp. 145–147)

1. Sea-mouse, *Aphrodite aculeata* : 3 or 4 in. 2. *Harmothoë imbricata* (a scale-worm) : ½ in. 3. Sand scale-worm, *Sthenelais boa* : 4–8 in. 4. Green paddle-worm, *Phyllodoce lamelligera* : to 18 in. 5. *Nereis pelagica* : 5 in. 6. Cat-worm or 'white cat', *Nephthys hombergi* : 6 in. 7. *Glycera lapidum* : to 4 in.

helplessly stranded on the beach : its sting can be very painful.

The commonest of the jellyfish—fortunately a harmless type—the moon jelly, *Aurelia aurita* (Plate **31**, *2*), is rather small, up to eight inches across, and is almost colourless except for four purple rings in its body ; tiny creatures from the plankton adhere to its tentacles and are passed to its mouth by the movements of its hair-like cilia. Another harmless type, *Rhizostoma octopus* (Plate **31**, *5*), is larger, up to about two feet across ; its mouth is divided into numerous small channels through which plankton are drawn by currents produced by movements of the cilia. The bell jellyfish, *Haliclystus auricula* (Plate **31**, *1*), attaches itself to weed, especially eel-grass, by a sucker on the reverse side from the mouth ; it is so delicate that its full beauty can only be distinguished under water.

## Comb-jellies

Although the comb-jellies (Ctenophora)—another type of open-sea animal sometimes left in the rock-pools—resemble the jellyfish, in many respects they differ from them. They possess no stinging cells, and swim by means of eight lines of cilia united to form comb-like projections (' ctenes '). Their eggs develop without any intermediate stage into young comb-jellies.

The sea-gooseberry, *Pleurobrachia pileus* (Plate **31**, *6*), over half an inch long, gets its name from its appearance ; in addition to its combs it has long tentacles with which it entraps its prey. The larger thimble-shaped *Beroe cucumis* is up to two inches long ; it has no tentacles, but its ' combs ' are plainly visible.

## Sea-anemones and other Anthozoa

When touched, or when out of water, the sea-anemones (classed, with the corals, as Anthozoa) contract into featureless masses of jelly, but normally when in sea water they expand what look like petals. In spite of their flower-like appearance, however, they are not plants but carnivorous animals. Their apparent petals are their tentacles, armed with numerous stinging cells ready when any small animal touches them not only to transfix it with barbed harpoons but to inject it with droplets of poison so potent that the victim dies even if removed from the grip of the tentacles. Though not large enough to hurt any but the most sensitive skin, their touch may feel sticky.

These animals have no medusa phase. Some produce eggs which develop into tiny polyps, and are either shed into the water or held inside the parent's body until they have attained adult form. Others also reproduce by splitting lengthwise into two or more parts, or by separating off parts of the basal disc to develop into small polyps.

The rounded fleshy animals called from their appearance and texture dead men's fingers or soft coral, *Alcyonium digitatum* (Plate **32**, *1*), are colonial Anthozoa. Their colour ranges from orange through yellow or pink to white, and they may be as much as eight inches tall. When out of water the polyps form small depressions on the surface of the colony, expanding above this when the water surrounds them.

Most of the anemones found on British shores are solitary animals. One type, *Peachia hastata* (Plate **32**, *2*), perhaps five inches tall, is unusual in that it has no basal disc ; it is not attached to any surface but burrows from a few inches to a foot deep in the sand or mud, usually near low-water mark. Its eggs hatch into polyp larvæ, and these are parasitic on the jellyfish, which disperse them over a wider area.

The other sea-anemones are fastened by a disc at their base to the rocks or other surface. The most common is the small beadlet anemone, *Actinia equina* (Plate **32**, *3*), which gets its name from the blue ' beads ' on its smooth body. It has a wide range of colours, green, yellow, brown, or red spotted with green. Perhaps an inch and a half high, it has about two hundred tentacles arranged in six circles, withdrawing them if touched.

The snake-locks or opelet anemone, *Anemonia sulcata* (Plate **32**, *4*), is also smooth-bodied, and may be four inches tall ; it too has about two hundred tentacles, but they are non-contractile and do not withdraw into the body even when touched. It may be purple-brown, pink or apple-green. This type really forms a symbiosis with the algæ it contains, and prefers sunny but tranquil rock-pools.

Two kinds of anemone have vertical rows of wart-like projections along their columns. The dahlia anemone, *Tealia felina* (Plate **32**, *5*), is

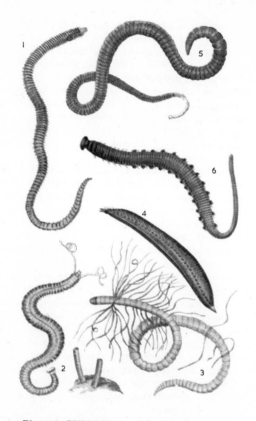

**Plate 36** BURROWING WORMS (pp. 147–148)

1. Rag-worm, *Nerine foliosa* : to 6 in. 2. Rock-boring worm, *Polydora ciliata*, with tubes : to 1 in. 3. Red-threads, *Cirratulus cirratus* : to 4 in. 4. *Ophelia limacina* : to 1 in. 5. *Capitella capitata* : to 4 in. 6. Lug-worm or lob-worm, *Arenicola marina* : 6 in.

fairly small; it has a base perhaps two inches across, and is about an inch high. It has about eighty tentacles, and is usually olive-green, possibly with red blotches, but these colours may be partly hidden by fragments of shell or gravel sticking to its warts.

The wartlet or gem anemone, *Bunodactis verrucosa* (Plate **32**, *6*), of the south or south-west coast, is perhaps one inch high. It may be recognized by its large white warts; it has about fifty tentacles.

The plumose anemone, *Metridium senile* (Plate **34**, *1*), gets its name from the feathery look of its numerous tentacles; these, however, develop only in the adult stage. Its colour varies from white to olive or brown and it is a few inches tall. It occurs not only in shallow water but in such sheltered places as rock clefts and among pier piles.

Two species are somewhat similar. The cave-dwelling anemone, *Sagartia troglodytes* (Plate **34**, *2*), favours rock crannies, some of which are filled with mud into which the animal can shrink; fragments of shell and fine gravel adhere to its body. The colours of *Sagartia elegans* (Plate **34**, *3* and *3a*) are brighter, and it does not cover itself with mud or other material. If it is disturbed white stinging threads may emerge from its column.

The daisy anemone, *Cereus pedunculatus* (Plate **34**, *4*), may be four inches high and have a slender stalk, which may widen out into a trumpet mouth; it has hundreds of tentacles, arranged in half a dozen concentric rings. It may protrude from cracks in the rocks, or from the mud, into which it sinks when disturbed.

The jewel anemone or globehorn, *Corynactis viridis* (Plate **34**, *5*), is quite small, only about half an inch across, and though it is not a colonial type its specimens grow so closely together that they might be mistaken for a colony. It is usually grass-green but may be white or yellow, orange or red. It has small knobs on the end of its tentacles, and though it has no external skeleton is more akin to the corals than to the other anemones.

## Anemones and hermit crabs

Two species of anemone are commensal with the hermit crabs, adhering to the shells which the hermit inhabits. *Calliactis parasitica*, which is pale grey or buff and has about three hundred tentacles, is usually found growing on the shells of whelks. *Adamsia palliata* wraps its base right round snail shells occupied by the crabs ; it too is pale, except for the magenta spots on its column.

## Corals

Corals differ from the anemones in producing ' cups ' forming an external skeleton of limy material. Except in a few places on the south-western coasts, where they are fairly plentiful, they are rare on British shores.

The Devonshire cup coral, *Caryophyllia smithii* (Plate **34**, *6*), fills a cup about three-quarters of an inch across ; when it expands it may overflow the cup and be mistaken for an anemone. Most specimens are white, but some are pink, and each individual coral has about fifty tentacles.

The rare star coral, *Balanophyllia regia*, is even more brightly coloured : a vivid orange or scarlet with transparent tentacles. It lives in deep sheltered rock-pools.

## WORMS OF THE SEASHORE

### SEGMENTED WORMS

There are many types of seashore worm, belonging to several distinct phyla. The *Annelida*, which include the earthworm of the land, have their body divided into rings or segments. Some creatures resembling the earthworm may indeed be found on the shore, but they are very difficult to identify.

Unlike the earthworm, most of the marine annelids, the bristle worms or *Polychæta*, have projections on their body from which extend a number of bristles ; the head bears tentacles and may even have rudimentary eyes. Some, living in conditions so muddy that there is a shortage of oxygen, have gills on their heads or bodies to supplement ' skin-breathing '.

Most of the marine annelids produce eggs which hatch into larvæ called trochophores (Plate **33**, *1*). After living for a time in the plankton, these develop into the adult form by growing additional segments, and then sink to their home on the sea-floor.

There are two main kinds of polychætes, the errant and the sedentary.

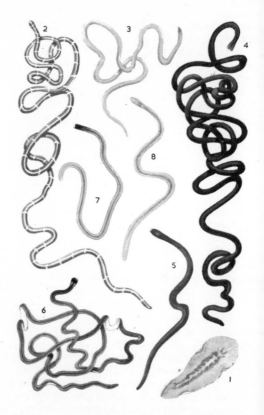

**Plate 37** FLAT WORM AND RIBBON WORMS
(pp. 153–155)

1. 'Living film', *Leptoplana tremellaris* : 1 in. 2. *Tubulanus annulatus* : 6–12 in. or more. 3. *Cephalothrix rufifrons* : 3 in. 4. Bootlace worm, *Lineus longissimus* : to 15 ft. or more. 5. Redline worm, *Lineus ruber* : to 8 in. 6. *Emplectonema gracilis* : 8 in. or more. 7. *Nemertopsis flavida* : 1½ in. 8. Pink ribbon worm, *Amphiporus lactifloreus* : 2½ in.

The errant kinds can swim or crawl more or less freely. In these the head bears a number of organs, most of them used for feeling, and may have rudimentary eyes ; the throat can be thrust out through the mouth and used for collecting food—there may even be jaws which can give the incautious investigator a nip.

## Scale-worms

Some of these worms, the Aphroditæ, have a body covering of large scales. On the sea-mouse, *Aphrodite aculeata* (Plate **35**, *1*), the scales are hidden by a mat of fine hairs, grey on the back ; the covering on its sides has been described as ' gorgeously iridescent green and golden hairs and lustrous brown spines '. This animal is three or four inches long and lives in the sand or mud at or beyond low-water mark.

Most of the shore scale-worms are smaller : *Harmothoe imbricata* (Plate **35**, *2*), for example, is only about half an inch long. It lives under the stones or among the holdfasts of seaweeds.

The sand scale-worm, *Sthenelais boa* (Plate **35**, *3*), may, however, be several inches long and is quite thin : the illustration shows only its head and tail. It has about a hundred and fifty pairs of scales and lives in the sand or below the stones on the lower part of the shore.

## Paddle-worms

The paddle-worms (Phyllodocidæ) are provided with ' paddles ' projecting from the body which enable them to swim and to crawl. The green paddle-worm, *Phyllodoce lamelligera* (Plate **35**, *4*), may be as much as eighteen inches long : it lives under the stones on the lower part of the beach. The spotted paddle-worm, *Phyllodoce maculata*, is only a few inches long and may be distinguished by the brown specks on its yellow back ; it lives among the stones on a sandy beach. The related green leaf-worm, *Eulalia viridis*, also recognizable by its colour, lives on the rocks and in their crevices.

The paddle-worms lay their green eggs in a jelly-like covering attached to the seaweed (Plate **44**, *1*). These hatch into larvæ, one of which is shown (Plate **33**, *1*).

## Rag-worms, etc.

The rag-worms (Nereidæ) have neither scales nor ' paddles ', and they can bite if incautiously handled. *Nereis pelagica* (Plate **35**, *5*), which is brown, with a touch of green on its sides, lives on the rocks in crevices or among the seaweed hold-fasts. *Nereis diversicolor* is darker, and has a red line along its back indicating its main blood-vessel. *Nereis virens*, which may be a yard long, is green, but with a pinkish underside and tints of purple on its back, and *Nereis fucata* lives in the shells occupied by the hermit crabs.

Two kinds of errant polychætes live in the sand. The cat-worm or ' white cat ', *Nephthys hombergi* (Plate **35**, *6*), is coloured light pink, shading into blue, and has a streak down its body, which is a few inches long ; when placed in sea water it

146

swims about. It gets its name from its head, which has two ear-like projections, and its long tail. *Nephthys cæca* has longer bristles and may be up to ten inches long. *Glycera lapidum* (Plate **35**, *7*), up to four inches long, also lives in the sand, but when disturbed rolls up into coils.

A somewhat different type of errant polychæte, the transparent *Tomopteris helgolandica* (Plate **21**, *4*), lives in the plankton, feeding on the other planktonic animals.

### Sedentary polychætes

The sedentary polychætes are so called because instead of roaming about in search of food they spend most or all of their lives in the tubes or burrows they have made. Their bristles and other projections are small, simply serving to hold them in place, but as the water in their lurking-place would otherwise get stale, they are able to produce currents in it by means either of their gills or of their cilia, or by rhythmically moving their bodies. They live mostly on planktonic materials, either gulping down the sediment around them and absorbing its digestible matter or obtaining it from the particles brought to them by the currents their movements produce.

### Burrowing worms

Of those which burrow into the sand, the largest of the common types is the rag-worm, *Nerine foliosa* (Plate **36**, *1*). Its body, several inches long, is reddish towards the head, green near the tail. The red-threads, *Cirratulus* *cirratus* (Plate **36**, *3*), up to four inches in length, lives not in the sand but in the mud, where there is little oxygen. Its thread-like filaments, from which it gets its name, are gills drawing oxygen from the water, and even when severed they go on moving.

The rock-boring worm, *Polydora ciliata* (Plate **36**, *2*), is able to burrow into the limestone rocks and the shells by means of a chemical its body produces. In sheltered places it may extend its U-shaped burrow by building short tubes of mud around each of the two openings, and from one of these it projects two vigorously waving threads—often the only part of the animal to be seen—that wash the water, with its oxygen and food particles, into its mouth.

Two species live on food obtained from the sediment, and their appendages enable them to make their way through it. The small *Ophelia limacina* (Plate **36**, *4*) occurs in large numbers in the sand, and *Capitella capitata* (Plate **36**, *5*), which looks like a short earthworm up to four inches long, with bristles on its first few segments, in the mud or muddy sand.

## Lug-worms

The lug-worm or lob-worm (Arenicolidæ), *Arenicola marina* (Plate **36**, *6*), betrays its presence to the fishermen seeking for bait by leaving on the surface of the beach a tiny pile of sand. This is so moist that it adheres to form a string-like coil; near by is a small pit, about an inch across, with a tiny hole in its floor. Coil and pit mark the two ends of the U-shaped burrow in which the lug-worm lives ; after swallowing the sand, the worm extrudes its inedible remains on to the surface.

The fore and mid portions of the lug-worm's body are much thicker than its rear portion, and from them project pairs of the red gill-tufts which enable it to breathe. Rhythmical contraction and expansion of its segments ' pumps ' water through its tunnel. Once safely buried it seldom moves ; even when reproducing it simply sends its spawn up through its burrow into the sea. A small annelid worm, of a different type, *Harmothoe lunulata*, may share its burrow commensally.

*Tube-worms*

Several distinct kinds of worm are able to build tubes, either of mud or sand or a limy material, or of a material secreted by their bodies. The tubes of the honeycomb worm, *Sabellaria alveolata* (Plate **38**, *1*), are so hard and so numerous that they may look like a mass of porous ' honeycombed ' sandstone (Plate **38**, *1a*). The worm that builds them is an inch or so long, and is red or brown, with a golden fringed ' collar ' and short thread-like tentacles. *Pectinaria koreni* (Plate **38**, *2*), on the other hand, can move about, taking its curved tube of cemented sand with it ; this worm, which may be two inches long, is pink and has fifteen segments with bristles.

Among the tube-worms are the terebellids. *Amphitrite johnstoni* (Plate **38**, *3*) is six to eight inches long, and has up to a hundred segments, of which two dozen may have bristles. Its pink-tinted body and its projecting orange or pink tentacles and dark red gills give it an attractive appearance, and small errant polychætes may share its slime-built tube as commensals. The sand-mason, *Lanice conchilega* (Plate **38**, *4*), is somewhat similar, but though its tubes, perhaps a foot long and a third of an inch across, may often be seen projecting an inch or so above the sand, the worm itself is very seldom visible.

Another kind of tube-worm is the sabellid. The peacock-worm, *Sabella pavonina* (Plate **38**, *5*), owes its name not so much to the colour of its body, pale green and tinted towards the tail with orange or violet, as to its crown of reddish-brown gills. These not only enable it to breathe but collect sand particles, out of which, aided by the slime it produces, it builds its flexible tube ; this may be eighteen inches long and extends a few inches above the surface at low tide. *Dasychone bombyx* is somewhat similar, but not so large, and its tube is only a few inches long and lies almost horizontally among the stones and the seaweed holdfasts. A shadow falling on to either of these creatures makes it take fright and withdraw into its tube. Still smaller is *Amphiglena mediterranea*, whose tube is only about an inch long ; this worm, which occurs in large numbers, and produces quantities of small transparent tubes, can leave its tube, and is remarkable for having eyes not only on its head but also on its ' tail '.

The serpulid worms build tubes of a limy material secreted from glands near their head, but they are also able to plug the opening, when they

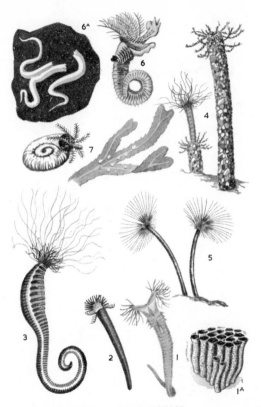

**Plate 38** TUBE-WORMS

1. Honeycomb worm, *Sabellaria alveolata* : 1 in. 1a. Tubes of
honeycomb worm: 1½ in.  2. *Pectinaria koreni* : to 2 in.  3. *Amphitrite johnstoni* (a terebellid worm): 6–8 in.  4. Sand-mason,
*Lanice conchilega* : seldom seen, but an inch or so of the tube
may be visible.  5. Peacock-worm, *Sabella pavonina* : 5 in.
6. Keel-worm, *Pomatoceros triqueter* : enlarged. 6a. Tubes of
keel-worm: to 2 in.  7. *Spirorbis borealis* : a number are shown,
at ½ natural size, in the drawing on the right ; an enlarged drawing
of an individual worm is shown on the left.

**Plate 39** BRITTLE-STARS AND FEATHER-STAR
(p. 159)

1. Common brittle-star, *Ophiothrix fragilis* : ½ in. 2. Black brittle-star, *Ophiocomina nigra* : to 1 in. 3. Daisy brittle-star, *Ophiopholis aculeata* : ½ in. 4. *Acronida brachiata* : ¼ in. 5. Common sand-star, *Ophiura texturata* : ½ in. 6. Rosy feather-star, *Antedon rosacea* (p. 163) : ¼ in. Sizes refer to the diameter of the disc.

withdraw into the tubes, by a small 'lid' which is a modified gill tentacle. The keel-worm, *Pomatoceros triqueter* (Plate **38**, *6*), builds curved triangular 'off white' tubes an inch or two long (Plate **38**, *6a*) on the stones and shells. Its body is purplish brown, and when covered by the sea expands a crown of red and white gills.

Masses of thin interlacing tubes coiled on the stones and rocks and seaweed holdfasts are produced by *Filograna implexa*. A coil, only about a fifth of an inch across, of a thin whitish tube on the fronds of the brown seaweed is that of a small serpulid : *Spirorbis borealis* (Plate **38**, *7*) when the tube coils clockwise and *Spirorbis spirillum* when it coils the opposite way.

## UNSEGMENTED WORMS

There are several distinct phyla of unsegmented worm ; not all of these, however, are marine, and most of the marine types are small and inconspicuous.

### Flat worms

The flat worms (Platyhelminthes), most of which are less than half an inch long, live mostly on the surfaces of sponges and sea-squirts or under stones, gliding smoothly about by moving the tiny hair-like cilia on their skins. Their mouths are on their lower surface, and they extend their throats through them to eat their prey. Their eggs either develop directly into the adult form or pass through a larval stage in the plankton.

The largest, the 'living film', *Leptoplana tremellaris* (Plate **37**, *1*), is only about an inch long ; the grouped black spots just visible on its back are its eyes. It lives under the stones, especially among the sponges. *Proscetheræus vittatus* is larger ; its off-white body is marked lengthwise by dark lines. *Procerodes ulvæ*, up to a quarter of an inch long, and with two blunt horns and two eyes, may be abundant under the stones where a freshwater stream crosses the shore.

## Ribbon worms

The ribbon or nemertine worms (Nemertini) have smooth slimy bodies, with remarkable powers of extension or contraction. They capture their prey, possibly as broad as themselves, by shooting out a long muscular proboscis from an opening above their mouths. The eggs hatch into *pilidia* (Plate **33**, *2*), larvæ which float in the plankton.

Some of these worms are devoid of eyes. *Tubulanus annulatus* (Plate **37**, *2*) may be as much as twenty inches long ; it is red or brown, and lives in a tube of slime under the stones near low-water mark. *Cephalothrix rufifrons* (Plate **37**, *3*) is only a few inches long, but it can contract until it seems little more than a thread or make itself quite broad ; it is pale with a reddish patch on its head and lives in clean sand, under stones or among the red seaweed or the shells.

Worms belonging to the genus *Lineus* are well equipped with eyes, though the dark colour of these makes them hard to detect. The bootlace worm, *Lineus longissimus* (Plate **37**, *4*), is incredibly long : a specimen is on record as having measured thirty yards and even then it was not half uncoiled ! Its blackish-brown body is usually found tangled together under the stones in sand or mud, or among the holdfasts of the oar-weed.

The red-line worm, *Lineus ruber* (Plate **37**, *5*), only a few inches long, also lives under stones, but prefers those on muddy gravel ; its body is pink. *Lineus gesserensis* is somewhat similar, but is green, and it is shorter and broader.

*Emplectonema gracilis* (Plate **37**, *6*) is another string-like form with a greenish, somewhat flattened body. It lives in the mussel beds as well as among the oar-weed holdfasts and under stones. The four eyes of *Nemertopsis flavida* (Plate **37**, *7*) are situated almost at the corners of a square ; its flattish body is over an inch long, and it lives among weeds and shells and under stones. The eyes of the pink ribbon worm, *Amphiporus lactifloreus* (Plate **37**, *8*), are arranged in four groups ; it is white or pink, with two darker pink patches on the head. Its proboscis bears poisoned spikes, but these are too small to hurt anyone who touches them.

# STARFISH, BRITTLE-STARS, SEA-URCHINS, SEA-CUCUMBERS AND SEA-LILIES

## ECHINODERMATA

The animals classed as echinoderms (' spiny-skinned ') are remarkable in possessing radial symmetry: they have no head, their mouths being mostly at the centre of the lower surface of the body. The body has a number—usually five —of parts so similar that when it moves any of these parts can go foremost.

They travel by the movements of their tube-feet, numerous small projections arranged in radial grooves on the underside of their bodies, and in some forms ending in suckers. The tube-feet are hollow and can be distended by water from the water-vascular system, one of the features which distinguish the echinoderms from all other animals. This opens into the sea through a perforated plate, the madreporite (visible on the back of a starfish), which conveys water throughout the body. Most of the echinoderms have limy plates in their skin, and some have the spines from which the phylum gets its name.

## Starfish

The starfish (Asteroidea), with its five pointed arms extending from the body, is very aptly named; at the tip of each arm is a small red eye, and beneath the body is a central mouth. It feeds avidly on molluscs (shell-fish), and if it encounters an oyster too large to swallow it pulls its shells apart and then thrusts its own stomach between them, thereby digesting the victim within, so to speak, its own habitation.

This makes the starfish a serious menace to the oyster industry. Nor can they be killed by simply cutting them to pieces and throwing the fragments into the sea, for if a starfish loses one of its arms it simply grows a new one. For this reason these animals may sometimes be seen with one full-sized arm and several small newly formed stumps ; then they are appropriately called comet-fish.

The action of the tube-feet can be seen by turning the starfish bodily upside-down and releasing it under water. One of the arms curls right over until some of its feet can get a hold—partly by suction and partly by a gummy fluid—on the surface below ; it drags the whole body over until the other arms can also get a grip and turn the animal right side up. Then one of the arms—it does not matter which—curves up, raising the eye at its tip clear of the sea-floor, while a few of its tube-feet extend as feelers ; the tube-feet on the other arms thrust it along, and the starfish moves with the raised arm foremost. To change direction it simply lowers that arm and raises one of the others.

The common starfish, *Asterias rubens* (Plate **40**, *1*), gets its specific name from its usual colour, red-brown. Its arms—normally five but in some specimens four or six—are tapered and their surface is rough with a line of spines down the middle. Its overall diameter is usually only a few inches but may reach twenty inches. It occurs on the lower part of the shore, where it spends long periods browsing on the molluscs.

The spiny starfish, *Marthasterias glacialis* (Plate **40**, *2*), is larger, up to about a foot, or less frequently two feet, across. As its name implies, its body, though rather soft, is very rough, and it sheds its arms if interfered with. It is most often seen on the west and south coasts of Britain. The scarlet starfish, *Henricia sanguinolenta* (Plate **40**, *3*), is smaller and has a firmer body ; it is recognizable by its colour.

Starfish with short, stumpy, blunt-pointed arms are sometimes called cushion-stars. One of these, the smallest British starfish, found only on the south and west coasts under stones and projecting rocks, is the starlet, *Asterina gibbosa* (Plate **40**, *4*), mostly an inch or so across (specimens are, however, known four inches in diameter) ; its body is very rough. Two larger types live beyond low tide level but may be cast up on shore. The duck's foot star, *Palmipes membranaceus*, has such blunt-pointed arms that it is almost pentagonal ; its body, red above and yellow below, is very thin and flattened. The pin-cushion star, *Porania pulvillus*, is thicker and its skin is smooth and feels greasy ; most specimens are bright red with white markings above and white below.

The burrowing starfish, *Astropecten irregularis* (Plate **40**, *5*), a few inches across, which lives not on the rocks but in the sand beyond low-water mark, is sometimes washed ashore. Instead of having suckers its tube-feet are pointed to enable it to burrow into the sand—an interesting process to watch.

The sun-stars differ from the general run of starfish in having more than five arms. The common sun-star, *Solaster papposus* (Plate **40**, *6*), which may have up to fourteen arms, is red or yellow above, off-white below, and lives on the rocks. The purple sun-star, *Solaster endeca*, usually has nine or ten arms and is named from the colour of its upper surface.

## Brittle-stars

The brittle-stars (Ophiuroidea) have small compact bodies, an inch or less in diameter, and long slender arms, which they shed very readily if, for example, they are trapped under the stones among which many of them live. Their tube-feet have no suckers, the animals moving by the sinuous movements of their arms. Their colours vary so much that they are difficult to identify.

The common brittle-star, *Ophiothrix fragilis* (Plate **39**, *1*), is recognizable by the five radial rows of spines on its body. The black brittle-star, *Ophiocomina nigra* (Plate **39**, *2*), which need not necessarily be black, most frequently lives among the gravel on the southern and western shores ; its body is so finely granulated as to feel smooth. The daisy brittle-star, *Ophiopholis aculeata* (Plate **39**, *3*), can be distinguished from *Ophiothrix* in having a body pentagonal rather than round that bears only a few small bristles, and by its thick shortish arms ; its disc is commonly red.

*Acronida brachiata* (Plate **39**, *4*) is recognizable by the contrast between its small body, about half an inch across, and its very long arms ; living just below the surface of the sand, it is commensal with a small scale-worm and a mollusc. The common sand-star, *Ophiura texturata* (Plate **39**, *5*), has shorter, stiffer arms.

159

## Sea-urchins

The sea-urchins (Echinoidea), unlike the star-fish, have no arms ; their compact bodies, which are almost spherical or heart-shaped, have radial grooves from which project the tube-feet which enable them to move. The living animal is covered with spines from which it derives its name, ' urchin ' being an old dialect word for ' hedgehog '. These, however, drop off after death, and the shell or ' test ' then resembles delicate basket-work. The mouth, on the under-side of the body, contains five sharp teeth, which form part of a complicated structure called ' Aristotle's lantern ' (Plate **41**, *1a*).

During the early part of the year the common sea-urchin, *Echinus esculentus* (Plate **41**, *1*), lives among the oar-weeds. Its nearly spherical but somewhat flattened body may be four inches in diameter and its test is reddish-purple. The purple-tipped sea-urchin, *Psammechinus miliaris* (Plate **41**, *2*), lives under the lower surfaces of stones and overhanging rock ; it is smaller, only about two inches in diameter, and may camouflage its body with bits of shell or seaweed. Two species are able to bore holes into the rocks : the purple *Paracentrotus lividus* on the south-west coast of England and the Irish coast ; and the greenish or reddish *Strongylocentrotus drobachiensis* on the east coast.

Other sea-urchins are denizens of the sandy coasts. One, the cake-urchin or green sea-urchin, *Echinocyamus pusillus* (Plate **41**, *3*), is oval, its

**Plate 40** STARFISH (pp. 156–158)

1. Common starfish, *Asterias rubens* : 6 in. (but may grow much larger).   2. Spiny starfish, *Marthasterias glacialis* : young specimen, adult size to 2 ft.   3. Scarlet starfish, *Henricia sanguinolenta* : 6 in.   4. Starlet, *Asterina gibbosa* : 1 in.   5. Burrowing starfish, *Astropecten irregularis* : 6 in.   6. Common sun-star, *Solaster papposus* : to 12 in., but usually 7 in.

body being only about half an inch long. It lives close to the low-water mark.

The heart-shaped urchins have no teeth ; their spines enable them to burrow into the sand, and their long tube-feet collect fragments from its surface and draw them down into the burrow to their mouths. The common heart urchin or sea-potato, *Echinocardium cordatum* (Plate **41**, *4*), two and a half inches long and sand-coloured, burrows down about three inches. The purple heart urchin, *Spatangus purpureus*, is rather larger and is distinguished by its colour. Both species are commensal with tiny bivalve molluscs.

## Sea-cucumbers

The sea-cucumbers (Holothuroidea), though vaguely resembling the plants they are named after, are of course animals, and some of them might be mistaken for worms. At one end of their leathery sausage-shaped body is a ring of tentacles ; these are really modified tube-feet, and any other tube-feet they may possess are short and stiff. Those found on the shore are small, the larger ones living offshore. When alarmed they may disconcertingly expel some of their internal organs.

The sea-gherkin, *Cucumaria lactea* (Plate **41**, *5*), is only about an inch long and has a thick leathery pinkish-brown skin and ten white tentacles. *Leptosynapta inhærens* (Plate **41**, *6*) is several inches—or even a foot—long ; it is pink or grey and has twelve tentacles ending in a number of branches, the outer ones being somewhat longer than the others ; *Labidoplax digitata* is somewhat similar, but it is reddish brown and its tentacles have only four branches. Both species are commensal with a scale-worm and a bivalve mollusc.

The cotton spinner, *Holothuria forskali,* a few inches long, brown above and a lighter colour below, has three rows of strong suckers and twenty short yellow tentacles. It gets its name from the sticky cotton-like threads which it emits when alarmed to mislead or entangle its foes.

## Sea-lilies

The crinoids or sea-lilies (Crinoidea) have ten feathery arms which wave in the water ; the hair-like cilia they bear produce currents which carry particles of food to the animal's mouth. Most live in deep water, and are rooted to the sea-floor by long stalks—hence the animal's two names, the word crinoid being based on the Greek for ' lily '.

A kind common off the British shores, the rosy feather-star, *Antedon rosacea* (Plate **39,** *6*), is however stalked only when young ; in its adult stage it can swim freely, making slow graceful movements with its feather-like arms, but it may be temporarily attached by its cilia to the stones. A curious rounded worm, *Myzostomum cirriferum,* lives parasitically on its surface and may be seen moving about on its arms.

# MOLLUSCS: UNIVALVES

## 'SHELL-FISH'

Two totally different types of animal are some-what confusingly called shell-fish. One consists of the Crustacea, such armoured, jointed creatures as crabs, lobsters and so forth, to be considered in a later section. The other includes animals having either one shell or a pair of shells; because of the softness of their bodies these, with some others that have no visible shells, are called the *Mollusca*, from the Latin for 'soft'.

The eggs of most of the molluscs develop into planktonic larvæ resembling the annelid tro-chopores, but in many the ciliated ring extends as a wing-like structure, and the larva is then known as a veliger (Plate **33**, *3*). In some of the shore molluscs, however, development is direct.

## Chitons

The chitons or coat-of-mail shells (Amphineura) are oval-shaped flat-bodied molluscs protected by up to eight jointed overlapping shell-plates. When the animal is removed from the rocks these fold to protect the body, which curls up into a ball. Like the limpets the chitons cling tightly to the rocks, though they are more difficult to see, being considerably smaller (about half an inch long) and almost the colour of the rock itself; they crawl over its surface, adapting themselves to its irregularities and rubbing the minute algæ away with their long tongues.

The commonest intertidal chiton is the grey

**Plate 41**  SEA-URCHINS AND SEA-CUCUMBERS
(pp. 160 and 162)

1. Common sea-urchin, *Echinus esculentus* : 4 in.   1a. 'Aristotle's lantern' (mouth of sea-urchin).   2. Purple-tipped sea-urchin, *Psammechinus miliaris* : 2 in.   3. Cake-urchin or green sea-urchin, *Echinocyamus pusillus* : $\frac{1}{8}-\frac{1}{4}$ in.   4. Common heart urchin or sea-potato, *Echinocardium cordatum* : 2½ in.   5. Sea-gherkin, *Cucumaria lactea* : 1 in.   6. *Leptosynapta inhaerens* : usually 4–6 in., but can be 12 in.

coat-of-mail shell, *Lepidochitona cinereus* (Plate **42**, *1*), which in spite of the name may be tinted red, brown or green ; its shell-plates have a dull look. The red chiton, *Tonicella rubra*, is more definitely coloured, and its shell is glossy. The bristled chiton, *Acanthochitona crinitus*, is named from the tufts of bristle on the girdle, which extends round the shell.

## Gasteropoda

The typical marine snail (a single-shelled mollusc) is a gasteropod ; usually it has a coiled shell which protects it from desiccation or other dangers. It partly emerges head first from its shell to feed and move, crawling on its foot— hence the term gasteropod (' stomach-footed '). Its soft visceral mass remains protected by the shell.

Within the shell the foot is continuous with the mantle, a layer of skin, which also covers the visceral mass. This mantle secretes the shell, and part of it may enclose the mantle cavity, which opens to the exterior and in most types contains the gills.

The shell assumes various shapes but is usually twisted into a spiral ; the result of this twist is that not only the shell but the whole body is unsymmetrical. Most of the shells have a right-handed twist, so that when seen from above they coil clockwise from the apex ; a few, however, have a left-handed twist.

The head has one pair of tentacles, and in most kinds has eyes. The mantle cavity opens above the head, and in some species the opening extends to form a siphon through which the animal breathes ; the shell is grooved to accommodate this. The foot may carry a horny operculum which closes the shell like a lid when the animal retires into it. Most molluscs have a toothed ribbon-like tongue ; the vegetarians use it for rasping food off the rocks, the carnivorous types for boring holes into their victims' shells and tissues.

## Limpets

Although its shell is not spiral but conical, the limpet's body resembles that of the other univalves, but its large sucker-like foot holds it firmly to the rock. If taken unawares, with its shell slightly raised from the rock, it can easily be knocked or prised loose by a human investigator or by the beak of a sea-bird. But the slightest warning makes it clamp firmly down, and then it will almost let itself be knocked to pieces sooner than release its grip. This protects it against the sea-bird's attack and the impact even of large violent waves.

When the tide is in the limpet moves slowly over the surface of the rock, grazing on the algæ but afterwards returning to the same resting-place. If the rock is not too hard it may wear away a hollow into which its shell fits exactly ; but it adapts the edge of its shell to fit a very hard rock.

The common limpet, *Patella vulgata* (Plate **42**, 2), has a tallish shell usually about two inches long, with a number of ribs radiating from apex to rim, and a white or yellow internal surface. When moving about the rock it projects its mantle, which is fringed with transparent tentacles, around the shell. The keyhole limpet, *Diodora apertura*, has a hole at the apex of the shell, and the slit limpet, *Emarginula reticulata*, a notch in its front margin. The kingfisher or blue-rayed limpet, *Patina pellucida* (Plate **42**, *3*), feeds and lives on the oar-weed ; the illustration shows both the immature form, which is marked with the blue lines from which it is named, and the adult in which they no longer appear.

The tortoiseshell limpet, *Acmæa testudinalis* (Plate **42**, *4*), has an irregular pattern of reddish-brown markings, and the inside of its shell is dark ; it is common in rock-pools and other sheltered places on the northern shores. *Acmæa virginea*, a smaller species found in the south, has a white shell with pink or brown markings and a light-coloured interior : hence its name, the white tortoiseshell limpet.

## Top-shells

The top-shells are recognizable from their shape and the tentacles which emerge from the sides of their occupants' foot. The grey top-shell or ' silver tommy ', *Gibbula cineraria* (Plate **42**, *5*), is about half an inch high and half an inch broad and occurs on the lower part of the shore. The flat or purple top-shell, *Gibbula umbilicalis*, has broader purplish stripes but no dots. The shell of the painted, large or common top-shell, *Calliostoma zizphinum*, is a taller and more pointed pyramid, perhaps an inch or more broad and high, with red streaks on a light yellow or pink ground. Even more decorative but smaller—only a third of an

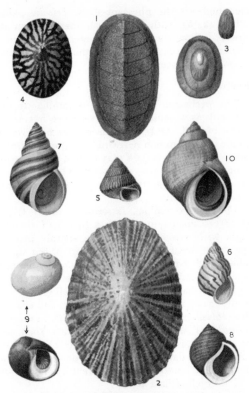

**Plate 42** LIMPETS, WINKLES, ETC.

1. Grey coat-of-mail shell, *Lepidochitona cinereus* : ⅜ in. 2. Common limpet, *Patella vulgata* : 2 in. 3. Kingfisher or blue-rayed limpet, *Patina pellucida* : young ½ in. (above), adult ¾ in. (below). 4. Tortoiseshell limpet, *Acmaea testudinalis* : ¾ in. 5. Grey top-shell or 'silver tommy', *Gibbula cineraria* : ½ in. 6. Pheasant-shell, *Tricolia pullus* : ⅛ in. 7. Chink-shell, *Lacuna vincta* : ½ in. 8. Rough winkle, *Littorina saxatilis* : under ½ in. 9. Flat winkle, *Littorina littoralis* (two varieties) : ½ in. 10. Common periwinkle, *Littorina littorea* : 1 in.

inch high—is the pheasant-shell, *Tricolia pullus* (Plate **42**, *6*), with its reddish markings on its glossy yellow shell and an operculum ('lid') whitened by a limy material; this shell is found among the red seaweeds.

## Periwinkles

The periwinkle—or winkle—is familiar to all, not only as a denizen of the seashore but as an article of food. Only one of its species, however, is edible: the common periwinkle, *Littorina littorea* (Plate **42**, *10*). It is dark grey or red, marked with concentric lines, and about one inch high; it grows on most parts of the shore, among the rocks and weed.

The rough winkle, *Littorina saxatilis* (Plate **42**, *8*), is smaller, usually less than half an inch high, with a rough shell and a sharply marked spiral; it occurs on the upper part of the shore. The small winkle, *Littorina neritoides*, is still smaller, less than a quarter of an inch tall, and is darker; it has a longer smoother shell and occurs in the rock crevices high on the shore, and even in the splash zone. The flat winkle, *Littorina littoralis* (Plate **42**, *9*), though larger than the small winkle, is only about half an inch high, and its spire looks flattened; it is abundant on the bladder and knotted wrack, where it lays its eggs in a blob of jelly (Plate **44**, *3*).

The chink-shell, *Lacuna vincta* (Plate **42**, *7*), belongs to the same family as the winkle. Its shell is small, about half an inch high, and is bright yellow, perhaps marked by red bands. It lives among the oar-weed, on which its eggs may be seen in a small yellowish ring (Plate **44**, *2*).

## Necklace-shells and cowries

Some of the gasteropods are carnivorous. The necklace-shell, *Natica alderi* (Plate **45**, *1*), burrows in the sand on the lower part of the shore. There it bores a tiny hole in the shells of the bivalve molluscs with the acid secreted by its body ; passing its proboscis through the hole, it emits a digestive fluid, afterwards sucking out the semi-digested mollusc. Its spotted yellow-brown shell measures something less than an inch in each direction, and during life may be partly covered by the large foot ; its name refers to the sand-stiffened strap-shaped coil in which it lays its eggs (Plate **44**, *7*).

The European cowry, *Trivia monacha* (Plate **45**, *2*), forms a shell about half an inch long, whose exterior whorl is so large that it covers all the others ; during the animal's life the whole shell may itself be concealed by the orange mantle. *Trivia arctica* (Plate **45**, *2a*) is similar in size ; it has a brown mantle, and there are no spots on its shell.

## Whelks

The shells of the whelks have long tall spires, with a notched opening. The notch protects a siphon which enables the animal to obtain clean water for respiration from above its head.

The dog whelk, *Nucella lapillus* (Plate **45**, *3*), is also called the dog winkle. The colour of its shell, one to one and three-quarter inches high, depends upon its food : when it feeds mainly on mussels the shell is dark, but when it lives on barnacles it is off-white or yellow ; a striped shell suggests that the occupant has had a varied diet. The whelk opens the barnacles by forcing their upper plates apart, possibly first killing them by the poison it secretes. (This is the dye purpurin ; creatures related to the whelk were the source in ancient times of the famous Tyrian purple.) Its yellowish egg capsules (Plate **44**, *4*), from which miniature dog whelks emerge, may be seen on sheltered rock surfaces.

The sting winkle or drill, *Ocenebra erinacea* (Plate **45**, *4*), can be recognized by the corrugations on its shell, which is whitish with dark streaks. Living down near low-water mark, it is a serious pest to the oyster-beds. The shell of the oyster-drill, *Urosalpinx cinerea*, which was accidentally introduced on oysters imported from North America, is less rough and its siphon is supported by a longish aperture.

The common whelk or buckie, *Buccinum undatum* (Plate **45**, *5*), is several inches high, and is deeply grooved ; it has a large mouth, creamy on the interior ; though the groove for its siphon is short, the siphon itself is long. It lives among the stones and mud on the lower shore, and its egg masses (Plate **44**, *5*) may be seen attached to the rocks or dried into a spongy material on the beach. The netted dog whelk, *Nassarius reticulatus* (Plate **45**, *6*), is smaller and slimmer, an inch to an inch and a quarter long.

**Plate 43** SEA-HARE AND SEA-SLUGS (pp. 174–175)

1. Sea-hare, *Aplysia punctata* : to 6 in. 2. Sea-lemon, *Archidoris pseudoargus* : 2–3 in. 3. *Onchidoris fusca* : 1 in. 4. Angled doris, *Goniodoris nodosa* : 1 in. 5. *Polycera quadrilineata* : ¾ in. 6. Crowned sea-nymph, *Doto coronata* : ½ in. 7. Grey sea-slug, *Aeolidia papillosa* : 3 in. 8. Crowned eolid, *Facelina auriculata* : to 1 in.

## Lobe-shells, sea-hares, etc.

Some of the gasteropods have shells so small that the animals are unable to retire into them or they are hidden by their bodies. Some have no shells at all.

The lobe-shell, *Philine quadripartita*, is common near low tide level where the sands are muddy. Its shell (Plate **45**, *7*) is almost completely hidden in life by the four greyish lobes from which it is named, formed by the head in front, the foot at the sides and the mantle in the rear. *Berthella plumula* (Plate **45**, *8*) lives under the stones, along with the sea-squirts on which it feeds ; its body is usually one and a half inches long, and its gill projects on its right side. The bubble shell, *Akera bullata* (Plate **45**, *9*), lives on muddy shores near low-water mark ; in life its foot has two mottled lobes which may either be folded over the shell or used for swimming, and its mantle projects behind the shell.

The sea-hare, *Aplysia punctata* (Plate **43**, *1*), up to six inches long, has a shell almost completely enclosed within its body and so thin and translucent that it may go unnoticed ; when alarmed this mollusc may eject a purple dye. It lives in the oar-weed zone, and in the spring it comes to the shore to lay its eggs ; these are contained in cocoons, hundreds of which may be embedded in a long orange ' string ' (Plate **44**, *8*).

## Sea-slugs (nudibranchs)

In spite of their forbidding name and the absence of a shell, the sea-slugs include some of the most beautiful seashore animals. As the term nudibranchs implies, they have 'naked gills', which in some types extend like plumes from their backs. Some are so small, or so much resemble the animals on which they prey, that they are difficult to detect.

The sea-lemon, *Archidoris pseudoargus* (Plate **43**, *2*), two or three inches long, is common on rocky shores. So, in the spring, are its eggs, which it lays in inch-wide 'egg ribbons' (Plate **44**, *6*) on the stones. It feeds on the sponges, and on the red sponges it may be red instead of the usual yellow.

*Onchidoris fusca* (Plate **43**, *3*), about an inch long, has an incomplete circle of gills towards the rear of its body; it inhabits rocky shores, feeding on the barnacles. The angled doris, *Goniodoris nodosa* (Plate **43**, *4*), has a smooth body about an inch long, with a ridge along its centre; living under the stones, it feeds on the sea-squirts. *Polycera quadrilineata* (Plate **43**, *5*), less than an inch long, may be seen emerging from the seaweeds. The crowned sea-nymph, *Doto coronata* (Plate **43**, *6*), about half an inch long, is splendidly camouflaged by the red markings on its pale body.

The grey sea-slug, *Aeolidia papillosa* (Plate **43**, *7*), is the largest British nudibranch, three inches or more long. It lives on the sea-anemones; not merely is it unharmed by the stinging cells of their tentacles, it can even transfer them to the projections on its own back, where they serve to protect it. The crowned eolid, *Facelina auriculata* (Plate **43**, *8*), has a similar mode of life;

it is smaller, usually less than an inch long, and is more decorative.

The sea-butterflies or Pteropoda ('wing-footed') are gasteropod molluscs specially adapted for life in the plankton. *Limacina retroversa* (Plate **21**, *8*) has a very small shell; some of the others have none.

# MOLLUSCS: BIVALVES

## LAMELLIBRANCHIATA

The bivalve molluscs are protected by a double shell hinged together and closed by strong internal muscles. Most of them are sedentary animals, either firmly attached to solid surfaces or burrowing by means of their powerful 'foot', and usually head first, into the sand or mud, or even into wood or soft rock.

Apart from the mouth the bivalve has hardly any head, though some species have eyes on the edge of the body mantle. It feeds and breathes by the stream of water which the movements of its countless hair-like cells draw through its body. It filters the water through its large plate-like gills, which not only enable it to breathe but also entrap edible particles from the plankton and divert them to the mouth. Hence the class name of these animals, Lamellibranchiata, coming from the Latin for 'layered gills'.

## Mussels

The edible mussel, *Mytilus edulis* (Plate **46**, *1*), has a dark blue shell two or three inches long and

**Plate 44** EGGS OF SHORE ANIMALS

1. Egg mass of leaf-worm, *Eulalia* (p. 146). 2. Egg mass of
chink-shell, *Lacuna vincta* (p. 171), on oar-weed. 3. Eggs of
flat winkle (p. 170) on *Fucus*. 4. Egg capsules of dog whelk
(p. 172) on rock. 5. Egg mass of common whelk (p. 172).
6. Egg ribbon of sea-lemon (p. 175). 7. Egg mass of necklace-
shell (p. 171). 8. Cocoon and ribbon of sea-hare (p. 174).
9. Eggs of sea-scorpion, *Cottus bubalis* (p. 223). 10. Egg case of
dogfish (p. 246).

**Plate 45** WHELKS AND OTHER UNIVALVES
(pp. 171, 172 and 174)

1. Necklace-shell, *Natica alderi* : ¾ in.  2. Cowry, *Trivia
monacha* (shell and living mollusc) : ½ in.  2a. *Trivia arctica* :
½ in.  3. Dog whelk, *Nucella lapillus* : 1–1¼ in.  4. Sting winkle
or drill, *Ocenebra erinacea* : 1¼ in.  5. Common whelk or buckie,
*Buccinum undatum* : 3 in. or more.  6. Netted dog whelk,
*Nassarius reticulatus* : 1–1¼ in.  7. Lobe-shell, *Philine quadripartita* : ¾ in.  8. *Berthella plumula* : 1½ in.  9. Bubble shell,
*Akera bullata* : 1¼ in.

occurs in such numbers as to form large mussel-beds. It anchors itself firmly to the rocks by its byssus, a bundle of short threads. These are secreted by a special gland in its foot and are strong enough to resist a forcible pull, but are attached loosely enough for the animal to swing round to meet the thrust of the moving waters with its narrower end. If the byssus be snapped the mussel, after drifting about until it reaches a new anchorage, can produce another; in muddy estuaries it may be attached to a stone, and if this is buried in the mud the mussel can cast off its byssus and grow a longer one. Otherwise, though while young it moves about propelled by its foot, when once anchored by its byssus it remains almost immobile for the rest of its life.

The horse mussel, *Modiolus modiolus* (Plate **46**, *2*), is three to five inches long, and is not so sharply pointed. It is a more solitary type, and uses its byssus threads to make a 'nest' of gravel and shell fragments.

The fan mussel, *Pinna fragilis* (Plate **46**, *5*), is the largest British bivalve, a foot or more long and six inches across at its broader end. It may be found near low water on muddy shores attached by its byssus to the gravel.

## Oysters

The edible oyster, *Ostrea edulis* (Plate **46**, *3*), has a whitish shell three to three and a half inches across, rough outside but smooth and with a slight pearly lustre within. It is a 'native' not so much of the shore as of the offshore shallows, where its large numbers form the oyster-beds; these are artificially cultivated as a source of food. When the larva settles on the bottom, the young oyster moves about until it finds a suitable surface to settle on, its lower shell being attached not by a byssus but directly by a cement; this cement is produced by the foot, which afterwards atrophies.

The saddle oyster, *Anomia ephippium* (Plate **46**, *4*), is smaller, less than two inches across: it differs in several respects from the edible oyster. It cements itself to stones, shells or seaweed holdfasts not directly but by means of byssus threads passing through a hole in its shell. It lives on the lower part of the beach.

## Scallops

The edible scallop, also called the great scallop and known in Scotland as a clam, *Pecten maximus* (Plate **46**, *6*), is another offshore mollusc, but its large shells, four or five inches across, may be found on the beach. Though attached by byssus threads when young, in its adult stage it gets loose and in an emergency swims freely by flapping its shells. It normally travels with the free edge of the shell forward and the hinge in the rear, but when alarmed it can retreat quickly, hinge foremost, by squirting out a jet of water; by ejecting the water downwards it rights itself if overturned. Unlike most other bivalves it has a line of eyes just inside the inner edge of its upper shell.

The queen scallop, *Chlamys opercularis* (Plate **46**, *7*), is smaller, two or three inches across, and both its shells are convex. Its numbers may be so great that they form a shoal.

## Cockles

The edible cockle, *Cardium edule* (Plate **48**, *1*), lives buried in the damp sand or mud of the beaches: a rich cockle-bed may contain over a million cockles to the acre. Its shell, an inch or more across, is more convex than that of most of the other bivalves, and the prominent ribs on the surface may enable it to get a grip on the sand.

The cockle's foot serves as a lever, enabling it to move over the surface of the beach : pressed down against this and then suddenly straightened it rolls the cockle over, and makes it leap into the air. By using it as an excavator the cockle can bury itself ; it then extends two siphons just above the surface, drawing a stream of water through one and ejecting it through the other.

## Wedge-shells

Wedge-shells live in the sand near low-water mark. The purple wedge-shell, *Donax vittatus*, is shown on Plate **48**, *2*. Fig. *2a* shows the interior.

## Tellins and furrow-shells

The thin tellin, *Tellina tenuis* (Plate **48**, *3*), has a thin flattish pink or white shell about three-quarters of an inch long. Its siphons are so long that it can live well below the surface. The Baltic tellin, *Macoma balthica* (Plate **48**, *4*), which may be red or white, is a denizen of muddier shores.

The flat or peppery furrow-shell, *Scrobicularia plana* (Plate **48**, *5*), is somewhat similar to *Macoma* but is larger, up to two inches long. It burrows more deeply in mud, generally that near fresh water in the estuaries; when the shell is closed its rear end gapes slightly. The white furrow-shell, *Abra alba* (Plate **48**, *6*), is small, less than three-quarters of an inch long; its delicate shell is translucent, and it too lives in the muddy sand or soft mud of the estuaries.

## ' Venus ' and ' Artemis '

The striped venus, *Venus striatula* (Plate **48**, *7*), has a shell an inch or so long, marked with over-lapping concentric ridges; it lives in the sand on the lower shore. The rayed artemis, *Dosinia exoleta* (Plate **48**, *8*), also lives in the sand near low-water mark; its ridged shell is larger, up to two inches across.

## Carpet-shells

The carpet-shell, *Venerupis pullastra* (Plate **48**, *9*), may also measure two inches across. Its convex shell is marked with concentric lines and may have irregular brown markings; because of its vague resemblance to the plumage of a hen it is sometimes called the pullet carpet-shell. Its hiding-place in muddy gravel or under stones or in crevices may be revealed by a jet of water when it withdraws its siphon.

## Trough-shells

The thick trough-shell, *Spisula solida* (Plate

**48**, *10*), lives near the low-water mark on sandy shores. Its heavy yellowish shell, marked with concentric grooves, may be about an inch and a half across.

## Sunset-shells and 'gapers'

A number of bivalves have shells that gape even when closed. The sunset-shell, *Gari depressa* (Plate **47**, *1*), about two inches across, is yellowish but marked by purplish or pinkish rays ; it lives on sandy shores near low water. The sand-gaper, *Mya arenaria* (Plate **47**, *2*), is larger, up to five inches long. It lives in the sandy mud of estuaries, above which its two siphons may just be visible at low tide ; it is edible and has been called a soft-shelled clam. The otter-shell, *Lutraria lutraria* (Plate **47**, *3*), is about five inches long ; it lives in muddy sediment on the lower shore.

## Razor-shells

The aptly named razor-shells live in the damp sand near low water, and may sometimes be seen just projecting above its surface, but when disturbed they quickly vanish into it. If the living animal be captured and placed flat on the sand, it at once digs downwards with its foot ; the moment it gets a purchase it pulls its shell upright, then it disappears with surprising speed, drawing itself downwards by alternately expanding and contracting its foot.

The pod razor, *Ensis siliqua* (Plate **47**, *4*), has a straight shell, six to seven inches long in the variety *major*, less than five inches in the variety *minor*. The shell of *Ensis arcuatus* is slightly curved and both forms have a cream-white foot. The sword razor, *Ensis ensis*, has a reddish-brown foot and is more markedly curved ; it has two varieties, *major* up to seven inches long and *minor* about three inches.

## Rock-borers

A number of molluscs can bore into the rock by rasping their shells against it. The rednose, *Hiatella striata* (Plate **47**, *5*), however, bores only into fairly soft rock, such as limestone ; on harder rocks it simply fastens itself into the crevices by byssus threads. It is named from the red tips of its two siphons, which may protrude from its hiding-place.

The piddocks bore into soft rock or stiff clay, leaving only the fringed tips of their siphons to project. The largest is the common piddock, *Pholas dactylus* (Plate **47**, *6*), up to four inches long ; on the back of its shell are four accessory plates.

## Wood-borers

Other types bore not into the rock but into submerged timber. The wood-piddock, *Xylophaga dorsalis* (Plate **47**, *7*), makes shallow rounded burrows in floating timber, and can withdraw into its shell, from which only its siphon projects.

The ship-worm, *Teredo navalis* (Plate **47**, *8*), has won notoriety for the destruction it causes. It not only bores into the wood by means of its notched shells but also feeds partly upon the material it

**Plate 46** MUSSELS, OYSTERS AND SCALLOPS
(pp. 176, 179 and 180)

1. Common mussel, *Mytilus edulis* : 2–3 in.   2. Horse mussel,
*Modiolus modiolus* : 3–5 in.   3. Oyster, *Ostrea edulis* : 3–3½ in.
4. Saddle oyster, *Anomia ephippium* (left valve above, right
below) : 1–1½ in.   5. Fan mussel, *Pinna fragilis* : 12 in.   6. Edible
scallop, *Pecten maximus* : 5 in.   7. Queen scallop, *Chlamys
opercularis* : 2½ in.

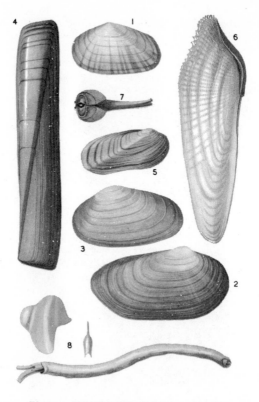

**Plate 47**  SUNDRY BIVALVES (pp. 183–184)

1. Sunset-shell, *Gari depressa* : 2 in.  2. Sand-gaper, *Mya arenaria* : 4½–5 in.  3. Otter-shell, *Lutraria lutraria* : 5 in. 4. Pod razor, *Ensis siliqua* : usually 6–7 in.  5. Rednose, *Hiatella striata* : 1½ in.  6. Common piddock, *Pholas dactylus* : to 4 in. 7. Wood-piddock, *Xylophaga dorsalis* : 1 in.  8. Ship-worm, *Teredo navalis* (with shell and pallet) : 6 in.

scrapes off, and meanwhile its worm-like body lengthens until it is far too long to withdraw into its shell. Two 'pallets' of limy material at the end of its siphon enable it to close the boring. (The illustration shows a shell and a pallet, as well as the animal itself.) *Teredo norvegica* is larger, up to a foot long, with a more solid shell. *Teredo megotara*, with an ear-like projection on its shell, may be found on floating timber along with the wood-piddock.[1]

## MOLLUSCS: CUTTLEFISH AND OCTOPUSES

### CEPHALOPODS

Though cuttlefish, squids and octopuses seem completely different from the univalves and bivalves, they also are molluscs; their shell, however, is very small or almost completely absent. Their foot is large in proportion to the body and extends to form a number of arms and a muscular siphon through which water can be forcibly expelled to give a jet-propelled movement. The arms surround the mouth, and near their base are the eyes. (Hence the technical name of these animals, from the Greek for 'head-footed'.)

The arms are mobile, and the hooks and suckers with which they are provided enable the cephalo-

---

[1] There is another type of bivalve which though formerly regarded as molluscs is so totally different in structure that it now forms a separate phylum. These are the brachiopods or lampshells. Though these animals were once so plentiful that their fossils abound in the rocks of Britain, they are now comparatively rare, and they are very unlikely to be found on our beaches.

pods to grip their prey firmly and drag it to the parrot-like jaws which emerge from inside the mouth to receive it. The continual movement of the arms, the throbbing of the body during breathing, and the grim-looking unwinking eyes give these animals an effect at once menacing and repulsive. Fortunately, however, none of those found on British shores is large enough to be dangerous.

## Cuttlefish

The cuttlefish and squids have ten arms of which two, the tentacles, are much longer than the others ; they are used for capturing food, and when not in use they are normally retracted ; only their broad extremities are armed with suckers. The other arms enable the animal to hold its victim more securely.

The common cuttlefish, *Sepia officinalis* (Plate **49**, *1*), comes inshore in summer to spawn in sheltered sandy regions. Its body is about a foot long and its back is marked with black and white stripes. When alarmed, however, it swims away and changes colour rapidly : it may change colour and then dart aside, squirting out, to confuse its enemy, a jet of inky fluid, the sepia from which it derives its generic name. It has a large internal shell which when washed up on the beach is known as a ' cuttle-bone ' (Plate **49**, *1a*).

*Rossia macrosoma* (Plate **49**, *2*) is found only on Scottish shores and is about five inches long. Still smaller is the *Sepiola atlantica* (Plate **49**, *3*), only an inch or two long. The common squid, *Loligo* *forbesi* (Plate **49**, *4*), has a slimmer, more stream-lined body with triangular side-fins ; its internal shell is a long horny ' pen '.

## Octopuses

The octopuses, as their name implies, have eight arms ; their body, which has practically no shell, is adapted not so much for swimming as for crawling. They may sometimes be found in the rock-pools at low water. The curled octopus, *Eledone cirrhosa* (Plate **49**, *5*), the most widely dis-tributed in our waters, has only one row of suckers on each arm. The common octopus, *Octopus vulgaris* (Plate **49**, *6*), with two rows of suckers on each arm, is restricted to the Channel coast.

## ARTHROPODS : CRUSTACEA

The other kind of ' shell-fish ', the Crustacea, form part of a large and varied phylum, the arthropods, named from the Greek for ' jointed legs ', which also includes the spiders, scorpions and insects. The bodies of these animals may be divided into head, thorax and abdomen and are segmented somewhat after the style of the annelid worms ; their legs, as their name implies, are jointed.

The crustaceans or ' crusted ' animals owe their name to the carapace or external skeleton which encloses and protects the soft bodies, and to which the muscles are attached. Their limbs are numerous and highly specialized for such functions as feeling their surroundings, fighting, shredding their food before it is eaten, swimming and walking. Their blood, being based not on iron but on copper, is blue, and their internal organs differ greatly from those of the vertebrate (backboned) animals. The stomach contains a ' gastric mill ' in which the food, already partly shredded by the claws, is pulped by teeth worked by powerful muscles, and the crustaceans will eat almost anything ; they have been called the ' scavengers of the sea '.

If one of their limbs is trapped, some Crustacea can bend it so sharply that it snaps off—and then grow a new limb to take its place. As the carapace cannot expand to accommodate a growing body, it has periodically to be shed ; and though later a larger carapace is produced, its owner takes some time depositing enough lime to harden it. Meanwhile the ' soft ' animal has to seek refuge in rock crevices, for it is now deprived not only of its defensive armour but of its aggressive weapons, which owe their effectiveness to their hardness.

## Copepods

The copepods are very small crustaceans so abundant as to form an important part of the plankton, where they provide food for many of the fish. The name, from the Greek for ' oar feet ', comes from their paired legs ; their head and thorax are merged, and the limbless abdomen ends in a forked tail. One of the most important is *Calanus finmarchicus* (Plate 21, 5).

## Barnacles

The barnacles, in their adult form, might easily be mistaken for small limpets, and were at one time actually regarded as molluscs. They include the multitudes of whitish shells, well under an inch across, which cover much of the shore. Inspection, however, shows that the structure of these animals is quite different from that of any mollusc : instead of being protected by one large shield-like shell, the barnacle has several platelets of limy material.

Still more do they differ from the molluscs in their development. Their eggs hatch into small planktonic larvæ, the *nauplii*, much like those of the other crustaceans, with a vigorous tail and a head with eyes and feelers (Plate **33**, 7). After moulting once or twice, however, these develop into the more specialized *cypris* larvæ with shells like tiny mussels (Plate **33**, 7a).

The cypris larva now drifts in the plankton until it finds a suitable rock surface. Settling down on this, it exudes a kind of cement which fixes its head to the rock ; then head and tail atrophy, except for the mouth, and the body develops its protection of limy plates. What had been a free-swimming creature spends the rest of its life, as has aptly been said, ' kicking its food into its mouth '.

The plates of the barnacle close tightly when exposed by the falling tide, retaining enough air and water to enable their inmate to survive until it is again submerged. In hot weather the multitudinous barnacles may close their shells so tightly, to prevent desiccation, that they produce a hissing or rasping sound. When the barnacle reopens as the tide rises, it protrudes six pairs of thin, curved, bristly legs, which set up currents in the water and entrap the plankton which this brings into their reach. From these legs comes the technical name for the barnacles, the cirripedia ('curl-footed').

## Acorn barnacles

The acorn barnacle, *Balanus balanoides* (Plate 51, *3*), less than half an inch across, has six protective plates enclosing a roughly diamond-shaped opening. *Balanus perforatus*, found on the lower part of the shore, has a taller, smoother shell, tinted slightly purple. The white ring which may be seen on the lower shore is the base of *Balanus crenatus*, remaining after the rest of the shell has been knocked away.

*Chthamalus stellatus* (Plate 51, *4*) is generally similar to *Balanus*, but the arrangement of the shells and the shape of the opening are different, and it ranges higher up the beach. *Elminius modestus*, with only four plates, is a recent arrival from Australia or New Zealand, presumably on the hulls of ships, and is now spreading northwards around the coasts of England. *Verruca stroemia* (Plate 51, *2*) has unsymmetrical white or yellow-brown plates and lives on sheltered rock surfaces and under stones near low-water mark.

## 'Barnacle goose'

The goose barnacle, *Lepas anatifera* (Plate 51, *1*), is one of the stalked barnacles, its long stalk

**Plate 48** SMALL BURROWING BIVALVES (pp. 181–182)

1. Edible cockle, *Cardium edule* : 1 in.  2. Purple wedge-shell,
*Donax vittatus* : 1½ in.  2a. Interior.  3. Thin tellin, *Tellina
tenuis* : ¾ in.  4. Baltic tellin, *Macoma balthica* : ⅞ in.  5. Flat
or peppery furrow-shell, *Scrobicularia plana* : to 2 in.  6. White
furrow-shell, *Abra alba* : under ¾ in.  7. Striped venus, *Venus
striatula* : 1 in.  8. Rayed artemis, *Dosinia exoleta* : to 2 in.
9. Carpet-shell, *Venerupis pullastra* : to 2 in.  10. Thick trough-
shell, *Spisula solida* : to 1½ in.

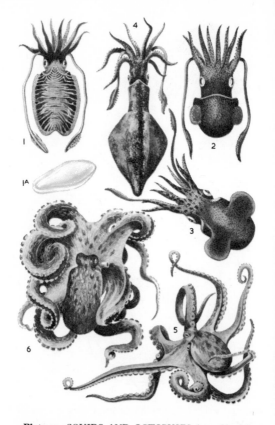

**Plate 49** SQUIDS AND OCTOPUSES (pp. 188–189)
1. Common cuttlefish, *Sepia officinalis* : 12 in. 1a. Cuttle-bone.
2. *Rossia macrosoma* : 5 in. 3. *Sepiola atlantica* : 1½ in.
4. Common squid, *Loligo forbesi* : 2 ft. 5. Curled octopus,
*Eledone cirrhosa* : 1½ ft. 6. Common octopus, *Octopus vulgaris* :
2½ ft.

attaching it to the hulls of ships and to drift-wood, buoys and so forth. Its triangular shell is almost white, and its stalk is blue-grey. Accumulating in large numbers, these animals seriously impede a vessel's motion, and it has to be periodically freed from them—nowadays in dry dock but formerly by the laborious method of grounding and careening.

In ancient times the belief was seriously held that the barnacle's protruding legs were those of a bird, and that the folded limbs within the shell were feathers. This, it was thought, was the origin of the ' barnacle goose ', which at last emerged from the shell as a fully fledged bird and flew away.

## Sea-slaters

There are many different kinds of small and inconspicuous crustaceans. The Isopods or sea-slaters are related to the woodlice. One of the largest is the common sea-slater, *Ligia oceanica* (Plate **51**, *10*), up to two inches long, with a greenish-brown body ; it lives in crevices during the day, coming out at night to feed. The gribble, *Limnoria lignorum* (Plate **51**, *6*), though only a fifth of an inch long, burrows in such large numbers into submerged wood that it can be very destructive. *Eurydice pulchra* (Plate **51**, *5*) is carnivorous, grey-green, and very common on sandy shores. *Sphæroma serratum* (Plate **51**, *7*) is found under stones and weed ; when disturbed it rolls into a ball. *Idotea granulosa* (Plate **51**, *8*) is common on shore seaweeds, varying in colour from olive-green to red according to the weed. Several related species are also common. *Jæra albifrons* (Plate **51**, *9*), so named from its white ' forehead ', is especially common among red seaweeds.

## Sandhoppers, sand-shrimps, etc.

The insect-like creatures seen hopping about on the sandy beach are not insects at all : they are included among a very different type of crustacean, the Amphipoda. The sandhopper, *Talitrus saltator* (Plate **53**, *3*), and the similar shore skipper, *Orchestia gamarellus*, some an inch long, live among the decaying seaweed. The skeleton shrimp, *Caprella linearis* (Plate **53**, *6*), half an inch or so long, is found among the living seaweed and is camouflaged to resemble it. The yellowish *Haustorius arenarius* (Plate **53**, *1*), found on coarse sandy shores, is adapted for burying itself in the sand. *Gammarus locusta* (Plate **53**, *2*) is typical of a number of similar species found under weed or stones. This species is a lower shore form ; some other members of the genus are associated with brackish water. *Corophium volutator* (Plate **53**, *4*), a burrower, is greyish and favours muddy sand or mud, especially in sheltered parts of estuaries, where it may live in great numbers and leave the mud surface at low tide punctured by innumerable pin-holes. When the tide covers the shore the elongated second feelers are used to gather organic debris to the mouth of the burrow. The wood-boring *Chelura terebrans* (Plate **53**, *5*), common in submerged timber, is always associated

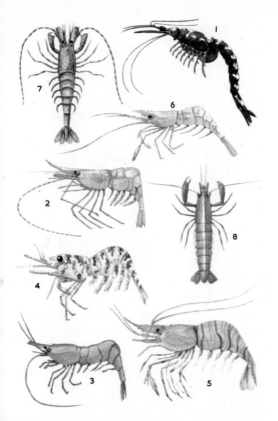

**Plate 50**  PRAWNS AND SHRIMPS (pp. 199, 200 and 203)

1. Chameleon shrimp, *Praunus flexuosus* : 1 in.  2. Aesop prawn, *Pandalus montagui* : about 4 in.  3. Chameleon prawn, *Hippolyte varians* : ⅜ in.  4. *Spirontocaris cranchii* : ⅜ in.  5. Common prawn, *Palaemon serratus* : 4 in.  6. *Palaemonetes varians* : 2 in.  7. Common edible shrimp, *Crangon vulgaris* : 3 in.  8. Hooded shrimp, *Athanas nitescens* : 1 in. or less.

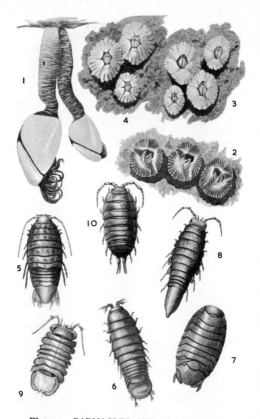

**Plate 51** BARNACLES AND SEA-SLATERS
(pp. 192, 195 and 196)

1. Goose barnacle, *Lepas anatifera* : 1½ in. 2. *Verruca stroemia* :
¼ in. 3. Acorn barnacle, *Balanus balanoides* : ⅓ in. 4. *Chthamalus
stellatus* : ⅓ in. 5. *Eurydice pulchra* : ¼ in. 6. Gribble,
*Limnoria lignorum* : ⅛ in. 7. *Sphaeroma serratum* : ½ in. 8. *Idotea
gramulosa* : ⅝ in. 9. *Jaera albifrons* : ¼ in. 10. Common sea-
slater, *Ligia oceanica* : to 2 in.

with the gribble (*see* p. 195), whose burrows it appears to use.

The shrimp-like creature *Nebalia bipes* (Plate **53**, *7*) is half an inch long. A carapace or shield covers the head and forepart of the orange-yellow or green-yellow body. *Pseudocuma cercaria* (Plate **53**, *8*) is found in muddy sand; it is one of the cumaceans, which are too small for further identification by the non-specialist.

## Opossum shrimps

The mysids are called 'opossum shrimps' because they carry their eggs in a pouch under the thorax; their bodies, which are less than an inch long and end in a tail fan, may bend double when these shrimp-like animals are taken from the rock-pools in which they live. The chameleon shrimp, *Praunus flexuosus* (Plate **50**, *1*), may change its colour to match the seaweed. The ghost shrimp, *Schistomysis spiritus*, is transparent and colourless except for its black eyes. The midge shrimp, *Hemimysis lamornæ*, which is less than half an inch long, is bright red.

## Krill

There are different types of the small planktonic crustaceans which form the krill on which even some of the whales live; they have a carapace and seven pairs of legs. The species illustrated is *Nyctiphanes couchi* (Plate **21**, *7*).

### DECAPODS

The larger crustaceans are known as decapods, from the Greek for 'ten legs', because of the five pairs of jointed limbs, perhaps including a pair of large pincers, growing from their thorax ; the first pair end in nippers, which may be quite small or which may form considerable claws. Other pairs of limbs, growing not from the thorax but from the head, are used in feeding, and further pairs, the swimmerets, grow from the abdomen. There are two main types : the swimming decapods, the shrimps and prawns, and the crawling decapods, the lobsters and crabs.

## Prawns

The prawn is most commonly found in rock-pools. The carapace, which covers head and thorax, extends forward in a beak-like projection, the rostrum ; there are two pairs of feelers, one longer than the other. The common prawn, *Palæmon serratus* (Plate **50**, *5*), the edible kind, may be up to four inches long and has a greyish partly transparent body ; it is most common on the south and west coasts, the east coast species, also edible, being the smaller *Palæmon elegans*. Still smaller, only about two inches long, is the *Palæmonetes varians* (Plate **50**, *6*), which lives in brackish pools in estuaries and salt-marshes and is almost transparent.

The Aesop prawn, *Pandalus montagui* (Plate **50**, *2*), is about four inches long ; its reddish-grey body is almost transparent, with red and black markings. The chameleon prawn, *Hippolyte varians* (Plate **50**, *3*), which is three-quarters of an inch long, gets its name from its changes of colour : in daytime this varies from green

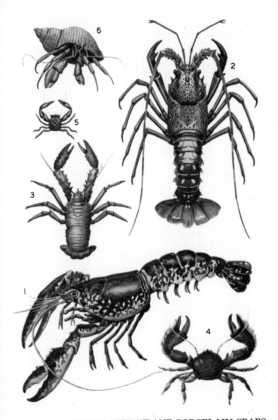

**Plate 52** LOBSTERS, HERMIT AND PORCELAIN CRABS
(pp. 203–204 and 206–207)

1. Common lobster, *Homarus vulgaris* : 20 in. 2. Spiny lobster, rock lobster or crawfish, *Palinurus vulgaris* : 24 in. 3. Squat lobster, *Galathea squamifera* : 2–3 in. 4. Hairy porcelain crab, *Porcellana platycheles* : 1 in. 5. Long-clawed porcelain crab, *Porcellana longicornis* : ½ in. or less. 6. Common hermit crab, *Eupagurus bernhardus* : to 3 in. or more. Sizes refer to body length.

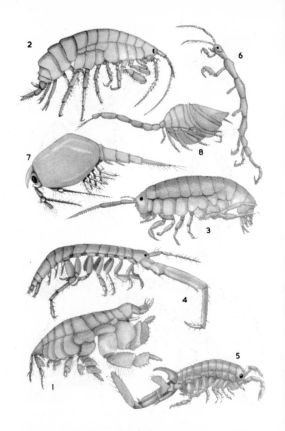

**Plate 53** SUNDRY SMALL CRUSTACEANS
(pp. 196 and 199)

1. *Haustorius arenarius*: ⅓ in. 2. *Gammarus locusta*: ¾ in.
3. Sandhopper, *Talitrus saltator*: to 1 in. 4. *Corophium
volutator*: ¼ in. 5. *Chelura terebrans*: ⅛ in. 6. Skeleton
shrimp, *Caprella linearis*: ½ in. or so. 7. *Nebalia bipes*: ½ in.
8. *Pseudocuma cercaria*: ¼ in.

to chocolate, depending on that of the seaweed it lives in ; by night it becomes a delicate
translucent blue. The larger *Hippolyte pri-
deauxiana* often has a light stripe down the middle
of its back. *Spirontocaris cranchü* (Plate **50**, *4*) is a
close relative.

## Shrimps

The shrimp resembles the prawn, but has only
one pair of feelers and no projecting rostrum ;
it is an inhabitant not of the rock-pools but of the
sandy beach. It burrows into the sand, leaving the
tips of its feelers projecting in quest of food, and
though another swimming decapod it more usually
walks on the surface of the sand.

The common edible shrimp, *Crangon vulgaris*
(Plate **50**, *7*), is grey or brown and is up to three
inches long ; it may be seen darting about in the
sandy pools, then suddenly vanishing into the
sand at the bottom. The hooded shrimp, *Athanas
nitescens* (Plate **50**, *8*), is smaller, only an inch or
less long ; it is red with a white stripe down its
back, and its claws make it look like a very small
lobster.

## Lobsters

The common lobster, *Homarus vulgaris* (Plate
**52**, *1*), is large—it may be as much as twenty
inches long—and is armed with formidable claws.
It lives on rocky coasts, but if found in a large
pool it is best left severely alone ; and if trapped in
a fisherman's pot it should be handled only by the
experienced. In life it is blue, the familiar red

colour appearing only as a result of cooking, though the smaller, slimmer Norway lobster, *Nephrops norvegicus*, is reddish even when alive.

The spiny lobster, rock lobster or crawfish, *Palinurus vulgaris* (Plate **52**, *2*), may be even larger, up to two feet long, but it has no large claws ; this also lives offshore or in the rock-pools. It is said to be able to produce sounds with the bases of its feelers.

The squat lobster keeps its abdomen tucked under the body, where it is almost invisible, and is smaller than the true lobster. *Galathea squamifera* (Plate **52**, *3*) is only two to three inches long, and its greenish-brown body may be flecked with red ; it lives under the seaweed and stones. *Galathea strigosa* is striped red and blue, and though it is not large, up to six inches long, one authority describes it tersely as ' fierce '.

## Crabs

The crab also carries its abdomen, its ' apron ', tucked under its body, which is protected, with the head, by its broad shield, oval or almost round ; the large fighting claws curve round the front edge of the shield, near which project the short eye-stalks. It can give an investigator's fingers a nasty nip ; and, if large and ensconced in a rock crevice, it is said to be able to straighten its legs so power-fully as to jam his hand between its carapace and the rock. With the tide rising this could be very dangerous.

The tiny larva from which the crab develops goes through several stages before it takes its adult form. Before they hatch, the female crab carries a mass of eggs between the underside of the body and the apron, and is then said to be ' in berry '. (A yellow object in the same position is the only visible part of the sac barnacle, *Sacculina carcini*, which is often parasitic on the crab.)

The shore crab, *Carcinus mænas* (Plate **54**, *2*), may be up to four inches across, and is dark green, though the smaller ones are more variously coloured. The edible crab, *Cancer pagurus* (Plate **54**, *1*), is larger, and may be eight inches or more across; its colour is pink-brown and it frequents rocky shores, where it lives under the stones and seaweed. Its larva passes through several stages, of which two, the first larva and the megalopa larva, which moults to form a baby crab, are shown (Plate **33**, *8* and *8a*).

The fiddler or velvet swimming-crab, *Portunus puber* (Plate **54**, *3*), is reddish brown, and its joints and legs are marked with blue lines; it is several inches across and is described as ' pugnacious '. It derives one of its names from the mat of short hair on its shell.

The masked crab, *Corystes cassivelaunus* (Plate **54**, *4*), is so called because of the fanciful resemblance of the markings on its yellow-brown shell, which is about an inch across, to a face. It is a sand-burrower, drawing water to its gills by holding two of its feelers together to form a tube, their tips projecting well above the surface. The furrowed crab, *Xantho incisus* (Plate **54**, *5*), is reddish, but its nippers are black; its shell, two or three inches wide, is grooved across the middle.

The pea crab, *Pinnotheres pisum* (Plate **54**, *6*), shelters inside the valves of living bivalve molluscs, especially mussels and sometimes cockles, combing filtered food material off the gills of the mollusc— an example of parasitism.

The hairy porcelain crab, *Porcellana platycheles* (Plate **52**, *4*), has apparently only three pairs of legs, a fourth pair being folded across the base of the tail. Its body, an inch or so across, is brownish, and mud which collects on its hairy claws helps to camouflage it as it presses itself against the lower surface of a stone. The long-clawed porcelain crab, *Porcellana longicornis* (Plate **52**, *5*), is smaller, half an inch or less across, and a shiny red-brown ; its legs are devoid of hair, and it is not so fond of mud. The larvæ of both kinds float buoyantly among the plankton (Plate **33**, *9*).

## Spider-crabs and sea-spiders

The spider-crabs and sea-spiders have little in common with the ordinary land spider except their names. These come from their spider-like appearance, a small body forming the centre for a number of long jointed legs. The spider-crab's body is roughly triangular, with the head forming the apex ; that of the sea-spider is long and thin.

The body of the common spider-crab, *Hyas araneus* (Plate **55**, *1*), is an inch or two broad at its base ; dull purple-red in colour, it bristles with a number of tubercles, hook-like projections to which the crab attaches fragments of seaweed, sea-fir or sponge ; these form an efficient camouflage. The nippers are sizable, the rest of the legs very thin. The scorpion spider-crab, *Inachus dorynchus* (Plate **55**, *2*), is smaller with a body about three-quarters of an inch across at its base, and lives lower down on the shore.

The long-legged spider-crab, *Macropodia rostrata* (Plate **55**, *3*), has a shell about half an inch across, and its long ' spidery ' legs are hairy. It lives under stones or among the seaweeds and swims in a slow undulating manner. The spiny spider-crab or devil's crab, *Maia squinado*, on the other hand, is quite large, its body being up to eight inches long with shorter legs, their span being something over a foot.

Even more than the spider-crabs the sea-spiders seem to be ' all legs '. The abdomen is only vestigial, and the male carries the eggs on one specialized pair of legs. *Nymphon gracile* (Plate **55**, *4*) has a body a third of an inch long or less, and legs up to an inch long ; it is pink or pink-yellow and lives on stones and among the seaweed. The greenish-brown *Endeis spinosa* (Plate **55**, *5*) has a body only a fifth of an inch long, its legs measuring something less than an inch. *Pycnogonum littorale* (Plate **55**, *6*), over half an inch long, is yellow or brown, and may be seen crawling over and feeding on the columns of sea-anemones.

## Hermit crabs

The common hermit crab, *Eupagurus bernhardus* (Plate **52**, *6*), is armoured only on the forepart of its body. It protects its soft abdomen by living in an abandoned shell, its claws alternately serving as a ' door ' and protruding for

**Plate 54** CRABS (pp. 205-206)

1. Edible crab, *Cancer pagurus* : to 8 in. or more. 2. Shore
crab, *Carcinus maenas* : 4 in. 3. Fiddler or velvet swimming-
crab, *Portunus puber* : 4 in. 4. Masked crab, *Corystes cassivelaunus* : 1 in. 5. Furrowed crab, *Xantho incisus* : 2½ in. 6. Pea
crab, *Pinnotheres pisum* : ⅓ in. Sizes refer to breadth.

purposes of offence, for this crab is very pugnacious; its well-developed legs enable it to walk about freely, carrying the shell with it.

When the hermit crab grows too large for its prefabricated home, it forages about in search of another. On finding a suitable shell it examines it carefully; finding it satisfactory, it quickly whisks its unprotected body out of the old shell and into the new.

Hermit crabs can form a commensal association with several other creatures. The brown-striped sea-anemone, *Calliactis parasitica*, is fond of making its home on shells occupied by hermit crabs; its poisonous tentacles form a protection to the crab and in return it gets some of the crab's food; sponges and hydroids may also encrust the shell. Within the shell, moreover, there may live a polychæte worm and a parasitic barnacle.

The hermit crab adapts its body to the shape of the shell in which it lives, so that it has a 'corkscrew twist'. So tightly does it fit the shell that it will break in two sooner than be pulled out by force; an observer who wishes to extract the crab may do so without injuring it either by holding a lighted match under the shell or by chipping its apex and 'tickling the tail' of its occupant.


## ARTHROPODS : INSECTS

Several kinds of insect inhabit the shore. One breeds in such vast numbers in the decaying seaweed that it sometimes becomes a serious nuisance ; it is the seaweed fly, *Cœlopa frigida* (Plate **56**, *4*). One of the commonest midges is *Thalassomyia frauenfeldi* (Plate **56**, *3*). The bristle-tail, *Petrobius maritimus* (Plate **56**, *1*), which may be half an inch long, can often be seen crawling over the rocks, in whose crevices it shelters. The spring-tail, *Anurida maritima* (Plate **56**, *2*), is smaller, only an eighth of an inch or so long, and its body is blue. It not only runs about the rocks but on the surface film of small sheltered rock-pools ; here it may congregate in such numbers as to form a large ' raft '.

There are also small shore-beetles, living under stones or in rock crevices. Two types are illustrated, *Aepus marinus* and *Micralymma marinum* (Plate **56**, *5*, *6*).


## VERTEBRATES : FISH

The vertebrates get their name from their so-called ' backbone ' or spinal column, which usually consists not of one solid bone but of a number of separate bones, the vertebrae ; it serves not only to give rigidity to the body but also to protect the spinal cord, an extension of the brain. They also have an internal skeleton, a head and tail, and limbs mostly arranged in pairs. They include the fish, amphibia, reptiles, birds, mammals and man.

The special features of the fish are that most of them are covered with scales and are streamlined

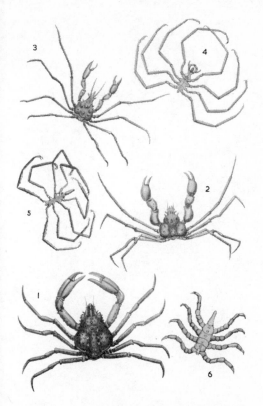

**Plate 55** SPIDER-CRABS AND SEA-SPIDERS
(pp. 206–207)

1. Common spider-crab, *Hyas araneus* : 1½–2 in.  2. Scorpion spider-crab, *Inachus dorynchus* : ¾ in.  3. Long-legged spider-crab, *Macropodia rostrata* : ½ in.  4. *Nymphon gracile* : ⅓ in. 5. *Endeis spinosa* : ⅓ in.  6. *Pycnogonum littorale* : over ½ in. Sizes refer to body length.

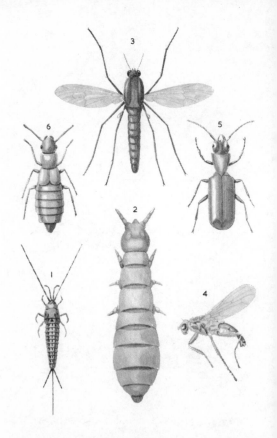

**Plate 56** INSECTS (p. 210)

1. Bristle-tail, *Petrobius maritimus* : to ½ in.   2. Spring-tail,
*Anurida maritima* : ⅛ in.   3. *Thalassomyia frauenfeldi* : under
⅛ in.   4. Seaweed fly, *Coelopa frigida* : ⅕ in.   5. *Aëpus marinus* :
1/10 in.   6. *Micralymma marinum* : 1/10 in.

to cleave the water ; the head and body merge with no intervening neck, and the tail expands into a large caudal fin. The limbs are fins, but not all of them are paired ; with the tail they serve to steer, balance, and stabilize the fish, which propels itself by movements of its body. Breathing by gills, it sometimes possesses an air-bladder which enables it to swim upwards, downwards or horizontally.

Some fish are adapted for life in the open sea, others for life on shore. Some of the latter have suckers which ' anchor ' them to the rocks ; others have flattened bodies, which can squirm into crevices or lie flat against the bottom, defensive spines or a protective camouflage. Most fish lay eggs which sink to the sea-floor or float in the plankton ; some of them after hatching depend for a time on an attached yolk-sac (Plate **33**, *10*). Many shore forms, however, have special means of giving their young greater protection.

## Pipe-fish

The pipe-fish (Syngnathidæ), which are related to the sea-horses, are camouflaged for life among the stems of the seaweed. They are propelled by the vibrations of their dorsal fin (the fin along the back) and feed on minute animals ; the eggs are incubated in the pouch on the male's underside. The worm pipe-fish, *Nerophis lumbriciformis* (Plate **59**, *1*), is found among the brown seaweeds : not only is it coloured like these but its body, a few inches long, feels hard like a seaweed stem. The snake pipe-fish, *Entelurus æquoreus*, is longer, two feet or so, and has a small tail-fin. The great pipe-fish or horn eel, *Syngnathus acus* (Plate **59**, *2*), lives among the eel-grass (*Zostera*).

## Sticklebacks

Though the casual seaside visitor may regard any tiny fish shooting across a rock-pool as a stickleback, the name is properly restricted to two definite kinds. The true sticklebacks (Gasterosteidæ) are classified by the number of spines in front of the dorsal fin. During the breeding season the male, which then turns a bluish colour, builds and guards a seaweed nest for the eggs. The fifteen-spined stickleback, *Spinachia spinachia* (Plate **59**, *3*), which is several inches long, lives in the weedy pools. The smaller three-spined stickleback, *Gasterosteus aculeatus*, two to four inches long, can live in fresh water, in brackish pools near high-water mark, or in the sea, though usually near the mouth of a stream.

## Blennies and butterfish

The blennies and butterfish (Blenniidæ) have a dorsal fin extending almost the whole length of the body. The common blenny or shanny, *Blennius pholis* (Plate **59**, *4*), is small, four or five inches long; it lives in the rock-pools on weedy shores, but may emerge to lie on the stones near the water's edge, supporting itself by its fins. Montague's blenny, *Blennius montagui*, is distinguished by its small red tentacles behind the eyes and its bluish-white spots; the butterfly blenny, *Blennius ocellaris*, which is up to seven inches long, by the black spot on the tall fore-part of its dorsal fin.

The queerly named tompot blenny, *Blennius gattorugine*, resembles the shanny but is larger, up to seven or even nine inches long, with conspicuous tentacles over the eyes. The eel-pout or viviparous blenny, *Zoarces viviparus* (Plate **59**, 5), is still larger, mostly up to eight inches but possibly up to twelve inches or more long; it is found on the weedy sands of the north and east. As its name implies, the mother retains the newly hatched young in her body, so that they are born as tiny fish.

The butterfish or gunnel, *Pholis gunnellus* (Plate **59**, 6), is a few—perhaps as much as eleven—inches long. It lives on rocky shores where there is much weed, sheltering under this at low tide but perhaps betraying its presence by flapping about; attempts to catch hold of it show the appropriateness of its name! It lays its eggs, as do the other blennies, in a large mass during the spring, but unlike the eggs of most of the others they are guarded not only by the male but by both parents.

## Eels and sand-eels

The eels (Anguillidæ) have a misleading resemblance to snakes; they are, however, fish, their head and tail blending into their long slippery body, and their tail-fins into the body fins. Their incredible life story is not yet fully understood: they lay their eggs in deep water in the Sargasso Sea not far from the North

American coast, so that the elvers (young eels) have spent nearly three years as frail larvæ crossing about 3,000 miles of the Atlantic.

The common eel, *Anguilla anguilla* (Plate **57**, *1*). spends most of its life in fresh water, but its elvers may be found on the shore, especially where it is crossed by streams. They ascend the rivers, in which they feed and grow ; those that survive return to the sea, where they lay their eggs and die. The males are something over a foot long, the females up to three feet.

The conger eel, *Conger conger*, is marine throughout its life but may be found in the shore pools, where it seldom exceeds one to two feet. Its dorsal fin extends further forward than that of the common eel, as far as does the fin below the body ; the body is grey-blue above and off-white below.

In spite of their resemblance to the true eels, the sand-eels (Ammodytidæ) are a very different type of fish. They swim in large shoals in the sandy bays, and may even be found buried in the sand. The lesser sand-eel, *Ammodytes tobianus* or *Ammodytes lancea* (Plate **57**, *2*), up to eight inches long, is greenish above and silvery along its sides and below. The greater sand-eel, *Ammodytes lanceolatus*, may be a foot long ; its snout does not taper so sharply and its dorsal fin starts further back.

## Coal-fish, rocklings, etc.

Several members of the cod family (Gadidæ) may be found in the rock-pools. The coal-fish or saithe, *Gadus virens* (Plate **57**, *3*), lives inshore when young. So does the whiting, *Gadus merlangus*, which has a black spot at the base of its 'fore-fin' and lacks the fleshy filaments on the lower jaw which most of the cod family possess. The pollack, *Gadus polachius*, has a protruding lower jaw, and the young of the cod, *Gadus callarius*, are marked with whitish spots.

The five-bearded rockling, *Onos mustelus* (Plate 57, 4), is distinguished by the two feelers on its upper lip, two by its nostrils and one on its chin; its young live under the stones and weeds in the pools. So do those of the three-bearded rockling, *Onos tricirratus*, which lacks the feelers on the upper lip.

## Flatfish

Several types of flatfish (Pleuronectidæ) spend the early part of their life on, or just below, the sand, and are camouflaged to resemble its surface. Here they acquire their typical form; hitherto like the other fish, with an eye on each side of the head, they take to lying on one side, the head becoming increasingly distorted, until both the eyes are on the upper side, along the middle of which is marked a 'lateral line'. Most are five or six inches long, though some are considerably larger.

The flounder, *Pleuronectes flesus* (Plate 57, 5), has rough scales along the base of its fins, and its lateral line is marked by small bony knobs. That of the dab, *Pleuronectes limanda*, is more distinctly curved, and the skin feels rough; the upper side is pale brown with vague yellow spots. That of the

plaice, *Pleuronectes platessa*, is nearly straight.
and the body is somewhat broader in proportion
to its length. Its young live in the plankton
(Plate **33**, *10*), their eye not having yet ' changed
sides ' to arrive at its adult position.

## Gobies and sucker-fish

The fins beneath the bodies of some of the fish
form a ' sucker ' which enables them to attach
themselves to the rocks. The gobies (Gobiidæ),
though abundant in the pools, are so small,
mostly about two inches long, that they are easily
overlooked. The common goby, *Gobius minutus*
(Plate **58**, *1*), though camouflaged to resemble the
sand, has a dark spot at the rear end of the dorsal
fin. The painted goby, *Gobius pictus*, is named
from the reddish bands on its fins and the black
spots at their bases. The rock goby, *Gobius
paganellus*, is yellowish with a pale band along
the top of its fin. The black goby, *Gobius niger*,
up to nine inches long, has a dark upper edge to its
fin. Unlike these, the spotted goby, *Gobius
flavescens* (Plate **58**, *2*), does not live on the bottom
but swims among the weeds in the rock-pool.

The lumpsuckers (Cyclopteridæ) have no
scales ; their sucker is easy to see, complicated
and very efficient. The lumpsucker, *Cyclopterus
lumpus* (Plate **58**, *3*), may be up to twenty-four
inches long but is usually much smaller. In the
spring the adults come inshore to spawn, the male
staying behind to guard the eggs and keep a current
of water flowing over them. In the summer, when
they are young, these fish, rather tadpole-like in

appearance and behaviour, may be plentiful in the rock-pools.

The sea-snails or smooth-suckers (Liparidæ) are only a few inches long. The common sea-snail, *Liparis liparis* (Plate **58**, *4*), lives in the rock-pools and under the weed; it lays its eggs in the hold-fasts of the oar-weeds. Montague's sea-snail, *Liparis montagui*, is marked not with lines but with dark spots.

Other scaleless suckers (Gobiesocidæ) are more common on the south-western coasts. The Cornish sucker, *Lepadogaster lepadogaster* (Plate **58**, *5*), lives in the lower rock-pools and often shelters under the stones; it is up to four inches long and is marked on the ' shoulders ' with two dark circles surrounded by off-white rings. The two-spotted sucker, *Lepadogaster bimaculatus*, gets its name from the dark ' eye-spots ' on its reddish body.

## Wrasses

The wrasses (Labridæ) are strikingly marked. The ballan wrasse, *Labrus bergylta* (Plate **60**, *1*), up to ten inches long—though some specimens measure sixteen inches—is common on most rocky coasts; it can be recognized by the white centres of its coloured scales. The cuckoo wrasse, *Labrus ossifagus*, is somewhat smaller; the females are mostly reddish, the males yellow-orange with blue stripes near the eye. The corkwing, *Crenilabrus melops*, is only a few inches long; it nests among the seaweed and its colour varies, but it usually has two upright rows of dark spots on the tail fin. The goldsinny or rock wrasse, *Ctenolabrus rupestris*, is reddish-gold ; it has a black spot at the base of its tail and another near the front of the dorsal fin.

## Sting-fish and sea-scorpions (weevers and bullheads)

While many fish have strong teeth which can give a nasty bite, others have a much more effective weapon, their sharp—and even venomous— spines. The weevers (Trachinidæ) are especially dangerous ; the spines which support their dorsal fins point upwards and are poisonous, even after the fish is dead : anyone who gets stung while incautiously grasping them or accidentally tread- ing on them needs, and should at once seek, medical attention.

The most dangerous is the lesser weever or sting-fish, *Trachinus vipera* (Plate **60**, *2*); it lies in the sand of the shrimping-grounds with its spines just projecting. Up to six inches long, it is grey or yellowish, with its foremost dorsal fin black. The greater weever, *Trachinus draco*, though larger, is not quite so venomous, but is none the less able to ' sting ' : it burrows in the sand rather further from the shore, so that it is less likely to be trodden on ; it has two small spines above each eye.

The bullheads or sea-scorpions (Cottidæ) get their names from their appearance and their sharp spines ; they are common, especially under the seaweed in the small pools on the north and west

**Plate 57** EELS, COD AND FLOUNDER (pp. 216–217)

1. Common eel, *Anguilla anguilla* : males over 1 ft., females to 3 ft.   2. Lesser sand-eel, *Ammodytes tobianus* or *Ammodytes lancea* : to 8 in.   3. Coal-fish or saithe, *Gadus virens* : to 40 in. or more.   4. Five-bearded rockling, *Onos mustelus* : 18 in. 5. Flounder, *Pleuronectes flesus* : 20 in.

**Plate 58** GOBIES AND SUCKER-FISH (pp. 218–219)
1. Common goby, *Gobius minutus* : 3 in.    2. Spotted goby,
*Gobius flavescens* : 2½ in.    3. Lumpsucker, *Cyclopterus lumpus* :
to 24 in., usually much smaller.    4. Common sea-snail, *Liparis
liparis* : 6 in.    5. Cornish sucker, *Lepadogaster lepadogaster* :
to 4 in.

coasts. They are remarkable for being able to make a grunting noise.

The long-spined sea-scorpion or cobbler, *Cottus bubalis* (Plate **60**, *4*), is usually six to nine inches, but may be a foot, long; it is brightly coloured and has five spines, the upper one long and rough. The masses of orange-coloured eggs which it lays in the late winter are guarded by the male (Plate **44**, *9*). The short-spined sea-scorpion or father-lasher, *Cottus scorpius*, is a little larger but not so brightly coloured, and has only four spines.

In spite of the similarity of name the armed bullheads belong to a different family (Agonidæ). The pogge, *Agonus cataphractus* (Plate **60**, *5*), is only a few inches long and has spines on its upturned snout; its eggs form a yellowish mass on the holdfasts of the oar-weed.

## Gurnards

The grey gurnard, *Trigla gurnardus* (Plate **60**, *3*), may be grey or greyish brown above and white below; it is seven to nine inches long, and is common in the larger pools all round the coast. The yellow gurnard or sapphirine, *Trigla lucerna*, is reddish, with some of its fins blue; the red gurnard, *Trigla cucurnus*, is smaller and more definitely coloured.

# VERTEBRATES : SEA-BIRDS

Birds still have a few of the characteristics of their reptilian ancestors, their scaly legs for example, but they differ from reptiles in being warm-blooded, and in having a body covering of feathers which enables them to keep their body temperature constant. They are, apart from the bats, the only vertebrates which have achieved true flight, and in most cases they are specially adapted for life in the air. The fore-limbs are modified to form wings. The feathers growing from the hand and wrist bones (the *primary* feathers) and from the fore-arm (the *secondaries*) are longer and stiffer than the insulating *covert* feathers, and, with the help of the tail feathers, they enable the bird to fly with accuracy and often great speed. The bird's bones are light and some of them are hollow. The breast-bone is keel-shaped, and attached to it are the powerful muscles used in flight.

All birds lay eggs and these are incubated by one of the parents, or sometimes by both in turn. The young are cared for until they are independent.

Some birds seen on the coast are equally at home inland, and this can be said of the so-called ' seagulls ', many of which even nest many miles from the sea. Some birds are only seen on the shore during periods of migration or in winter, and there are several which live well out at sea and only seek land in order to breed. There are indeed relatively few species which spend all the year on our coasts.

## Gulls

Gulls are the most obvious and familiar of coastal birds. They nest in colonies and, with the exception of the kittiwake, consume a wide variety

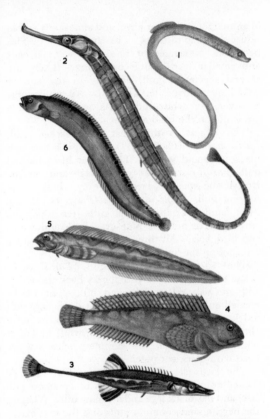

**Plate 59** PIPE-FISH, STICKLEBACK AND BLENNIES
(pp. 213–215)

1. Worm pipe-fish, *Nerophis lumbriciformis* : about 4½ in.
2. Great pipe-fish or horn eel, *Syngnathus acus* : about 20 in.
3. Fifteen-spined stickleback, *Spinachia spinachia* : 4½ in.
4. Common blenny or shanny, *Blennius pholis* : 4 or 5 in. 5. Eel-
pout or viviparous blenny, *Zoarces viviparus* : to 12 in. or more.
6. Butterfish or gunnel, *Pholis gunnellus* : to 11 in.

P

of animal food, dead or alive, and almost any edible refuse they can pick up. The larger gulls, besides being the ' scavengers of the shore ', will take eggs and smaller birds, adult or young. There are several species of gull, differing in size and in colour of plumage, leg and bill. All adult gulls, however, have white underparts, and most of them are white on the head and neck.

The largest is the great black-backed gull, *Larus marinus* (Plate **61**, *1*), with pink legs and black back and wings. The lesser black-backed gull, *Larus fuscus*, has yellow legs and, in the British sub-species, dark slate-grey wings. The herring gull, *Larus argentatus* (Plate **61**, *2*), the most familiar of the coastal gulls, resembles the latter in size but has blue-grey back and wings and pink legs. All three have yellow bills with a red spot on the lower half.

The so-called common gull, *Larus canus* (Plate **61**, *3*), is smaller with a grey back and wings and greenish yellow legs and bill. The black-headed gull, *Larus ridibundus*, is still smaller, with red legs and bill. In the nesting season it has a chocolate-brown (not black) hood, while in winter plumage, assumed in late summer, it has a white head with black ear-patches.

The kittiwake, *Rissa tridactyla* (Plate **61**, *4*), named from its peculiar cry, is of common gull size, and has black legs and a yellow bill. Whereas the herring and common gulls and the two black-backs have wings tipped with black and white, the tips of the kittiwake's wings are completely black.

Immature gulls, although the same size as the adults, are quite differently coloured, showing varying amounts of brown in the plumage according to species, and their bills are in most cases very dark-coloured, almost black, at first. Juvenile herring gulls (Plate **61**, *2a*) and lesser black-backs, in their first plumage, are generally considered to be indistinguishable. Immature kittiwakes have a diagonal black band across the wing.

## Terns

Terns, summer visitors to Britain, are related to gulls, but are smaller and more streamlined. They have black-capped heads and the feathers of their forked tails are in some cases developed into long streamers, earning the birds the name of ' sea swallows '. When seeking food terns fly slowly over the water, plunging at intervals to catch their prey (sand-eels are a favourite) beneath the surface. Sometimes they hover before dropping. Terns nest gregariously on the ground, and their eggs and young are so well camouflaged that many nests are trampled accidentally every year by unwary holiday-makers. The adult birds, however, usually advertise the fact that they are nesting by calling noisily and swooping fearlessly at intruders.

The common tern, *Sterna hirundo* (Plate **61**, *5*), is the species usually met, and during the nesting season has a vermilion-red bill with a black tip. The Arctic tern, *Sterna macrura*, is very similar, but has a completely blood-red bill and slightly longer tail streamers. The rarer roseate tern,

*Sterna dougallii*, is of about the same size, but has even longer streamers, appears whiter than the other two, and has a black bill with a red base. The Sandwich tern, *Sterna sandvicensis* (Plate **61**, *6*), is the largest of the commoner British terns—slightly larger than the black-headed gull—has a black bill with a yellow tip, and long feathers on its black crown which are raised in excitement to form a shaggy crest. The little tern, *Sterna albifrons*, our smallest species, is well distributed round our coasts, and is the only British tern with a white forehead in the nesting season. It has a yellow bill with a black tip.

Tern identification presents difficulties as bill colour can only be seen under good conditions, and in late summer common and Arctic terns are practically indistinguishable, both then having white foreheads and black bills.

## Skuas

Skuas, which resemble large dark gulls, obtain their food by piracy, forcing terns and gulls to drop or disgorge their catches and snatching them as they fall. They are seen mainly in the north of Britain, but are regularly observed further south during their autumn passage. Like terns they try to drive intruders from their nesting-grounds.

Two species breed here, the great skua, *Stercorarius skua*, a brown bird, larger than a herring gull, with a white patch on each wing, and the smaller, more graceful Arctic skua, *Stercorarius parasiticus* (Plate **61**, *7*), which also has white wing patches but has a very different tail; the

**Plate 60** WRASSE, WEEVER, GURNARD AND
BULLHEADS (pp. 219, 220 and 223)

1. Ballan wrasse, *Labrus bergylta* : to 10 in. or more.  2. Lesser
weever or sting-fish, *Trachinus vipera* : 6 in.  3. Grey gurnard,
*Trigla gurnardus* : 7–9 in.  4. Long-spined sea-scorpion or
cobbler, *Cottus bubalis* : usually 6–9 in.  5. Armed bullhead or
pogge, *Agonus cataphractus* : 5 in.

**Plate 61** GULLS, TERNS AND SKUA (pp. 226–228)

1. Great black-backed gull, *Larus marinus* : 29 in. 2. Herring gull, *Larus argentatus* : 22 in. 2a. Juvenile. 3. Common gull, *Larus canus* : 16 in. 4. Kittiwake, *Rissa tridactyla* : 16 in. 5. Common tern, *Sterna hirundo* : 14 in. 6. Sandwich tern, *Sterna sandvicensis* : 16 in. 7. Arctic skua, *Stercorarius parasiticus* : 18 in.

two central feathers project a few inches beyond the others. Arctic skuas are not all alike in plumage. Some are almost uniformly dark brown (the dark phase) while others have white underparts, tinged with yellow on the neck, and a black cap (the light phase). Dark phase birds are commoner in Britain.

## Auks

The auks are black and white, somewhat resembling penguins but unlike them capable of flight. They swim under water to catch their food, mainly fish. Four species breed in Britain, the guillemot, razorbill, black guillemot and puffin.

The puffin, *Fratercula arctica* (Plate **63**, *5*), is distinguishable in summer by its white cheeks, and these with its brightly coloured parrot-like bill give it a rather comical clown-like appearance. It nests in clefts or rabbit burrows.

Razorbills and guillemots nest on the cliffs, the latter often crowding together in large numbers jostling for space. Like all auks they stand upright, but shuffle about on their ankle joints rather than on their toes. The guillemot, *Uria aalge* (Plate **63**, *3*), which chooses the more open ledges, is dark brown rather than black and has a slender black bill. The razorbill, *Alca torda* (Plate **63**, *4*), is darker and has a deeper, sideways flattened black bill marked with a white stripe. The black guillemot, *Cepphus grylle*, is smaller and less common than either the guillemot or the razorbill. It occurs mainly on the coasts of Scotland and

Ireland, nesting usually in crevices or under boulders at the base of cliffs or on islands. It can be recognized in summer by its black plumage which is only relieved by the large white patch on the wing. In winter it has white underparts and is mottled black and white above. Adult birds have bright red feet at all seasons.

## Pelican family

Although true pelicans are not seen in Britain in a wild state, they have close relatives around our coasts. Of these the cormorant, *Phalacrocorax carbo* (Plate 63, *2*), is perhaps the best known : a large powerful bird, three feet long, with a longish neck and hooked bill. It spends much of its time standing upright on rocks, buoys or other objects rising from or floating on the water, with its wings held out as though to dry. From a distance it looks black, but its cheeks and chin are white, and there is a white patch on the thighs during the breeding season. Immature birds have whitish underparts. The cormorant flies purposefully, neck stretched out in the way that a duck flies. It can only really be confused, however, with its smaller relative, the shag, *Phalacrocorax aristotelis*.

The shag's plumage has a greenish gloss—hence its alternative name of green cormorant—and in the breeding season it can be distinguished by the prominent crest on its head. Like the cormorant it is a fish-eater, pursuing its prey under water, but it is strictly a maritime bird whereas cormorants often frequent inland waters. Shags frequent the cliffs favoured by auks and kittiwakes, while cormorants prefer small rocky islands for nesting and spend much time on sandbanks and estuaries.

An adult gannet, *Sula bassana* (Plate **63**, *1*), might be mistaken for a gull when in flight. It is all white except for its black wing-tips and its cream-coloured head and neck. It is, however, larger and has longer and more pointed wings than any British gull, and its tail looks pointed in flight. When fishing it dives from a great height, closing its wings and making a spectacular plunge to the water, sometimes almost vertically but more often obliquely. Gannets nest communally, usually on cliffs and rock stacks, and most of those frequenting European waters breed off the British coasts. Most of the gannetries are off the north of Scotland, but there is a large one near the Firth of Forth, on the Bass Rock, and another on Grassholm off the Pembrokeshire coast.

## Waders

Several species of wading bird frequent the coastal estuaries and beaches, especially when migrating. Most of them have a long bill, for probing the mud, and many have long or rather long legs. They spend much time feeding in shallow pools and at the water's edge, and outside the nesting season many of them form large flocks. They may be distinguished from one another by size, length and shape of bill, their differing wing patterns, and their call-notes.

The oystercatcher, *Hæmatopus ostralegus* (Plate **62**, *1*), with its large size (about eighteen inches) and characteristic black and white plumage, is probably the easiest wader to recognize. It is usually found on sandy or shingly shores, but in Scotland it also nests well inland. It uses its long orange bill not only for probing the mud but also for opening molluscs or knocking them off the rocks. In spite of its name it does not ' catch ' oysters !

The curlew, *Numenius arquata* (Plate **62**, *4*), is our largest wader, nearly two feet long, including its five-inch down-curved bill. It has brown, streaky plumage, and in flight it shows uniformly coloured wings and a white rump. Its beautiful call-note, familiarized by the B.B.C., immediately distinguishes it from the only bird with which it may be confused, the whimbrel, *Numenius phæopus*. The whimbrel resembles a small curlew, but has two distinct dark stripes on its crown and has a rapid whinnying note. It occurs mainly on passage. The curlew usually breeds inland, especially on moorland, but outside the breeding season spends much time on the coast, particularly estuaries and mud-flats, using its long sensitive bill to probe in quest of burrowing bivalves and worms.

The godwits are smaller than the curlews, but are still large for waders. They too frequent the mud-flats, occurring mainly on passage to and from their breeding-grounds. The black-tailed godwit, *Limosa limosa*, is a long-legged, straight-billed bird with a prominent white bar across each wing. The slightly shorter-legged bar-tailed godwit, *Limosa lapponica* (Plate **62**, *5*), breeds in

**Plate 62** WADERS

1. Oystercatcher, *Haematopus ostralegus* : 17 in.  2. Ringed plover, *Charadrius hiaticula* : 7½ in.  3. Turnstone, *Arenaria interpres* : 9 in.  4. Curlew, *Numenius arquata* : 23 in.  5. Bar-tailed godwit, *Limosa lapponica* : 15 in.  6. Redshank, *Tringa totanus* : 11 in.  7. Knot, *Calidris canutus* : 10 in.  8. Dunlin, *Calidris alpina* : 7 in.

**Plate 63** BIRDS OF CLIFFS, ISLANDS AND OPEN SEA
(pp. 231–233)

1. Gannet, *Sula bassana* : 36 in. 2. Cormorant, *Phalacrocorax carbo* : 36 in. 3. Guillemot, *Uria aalge* : 16½ in. 4. Razorbill, *Alca torda* : 16 in. 5. Puffin, *Fratercula arctica* : 12 in. 6. Storm petrel, *Hydrobates pelagicus* : 6 in. 7. Manx shearwater, *Procellaria puffinus* : 14 in. 8. Fulmar, *Fulmarus glacialis* : 18½ in.

the Arctic and has a slightly upturned bill and no wing bar.

The redshank, *Tringa totanus* (Plate **62**, *6*), is a bird of salt-marshes and estuaries, although it also breeds inland. It gets its name from the colour of its legs, but as these are difficult to see from a distance it is best recognized by its trisyllabic whistle and the white it shows in flight on the hinder part of its wing. The greenshank, *Tringa nebularia*, is seen on passage. It has greenish legs, longer than a redshank's, but is more easily recognized by its paler, greyer appearance, the absence of white in the wing, and its white back and rump.

Smaller waders include the turnstone, *Arenaria interpres* (Plate **62**, *3*), which owes its name to its habit of searching for food not only in rock crannies but on the beaches, where it overturns pebbles, seaweed and shell fragments in search of amphipods, molluscs, etc. It is a stocky bird, black, brown and white, with rich chestnut on its upper parts in summer, relatively short-billed and with short orange legs.

The ringed plover, *Charadrius hiaticula* (Plate **62**, *2*), is a plump little bird which gets its name from its white collar and black gorget; its back and wings are brown and its underparts white. It has the short bill and high forehead characteristic of the plovers, as well as their typical habit of running a few paces and tilting forward when feeding. It lives and nests on sandy or shingly shores, feeding mainly on molluscs, crustaceans and insects.

Other small waders occur in large flocks on the coast, numbers of them flying together with uncanny precision of movement. Among these is the knot, *Calidris canutus* (Plate **62**, *7*), which breeds in the Arctic and is seen here, usually in dense flocks, mainly in winter and on passage. It is a stocky bird, grey above and white below in winter plumage, developing rufous underparts at the approach of the breeding season.

The commonest small wader seen on the coast is the dunlin, *Calidris alpina* (Plate **62**, *8*). It nests mainly on wet moorland, but occurs on the coast in enormous numbers outside the breeding season. About seven inches long, with a straight or slightly down-curved bill, it is grey above and white below in winter, and reddish brown above in summer, with a large dark patch on its underparts.

The slightly larger sanderling, *Crocethia alba*, is one of the most active of small waders, and in winter or during migration periods small flocks may be seen at the water's edge, running in and out with the waves. In winter dress it is the whitest of small waders, pale grey above with a white head and underparts; in summer plumage its head, breast and back are reddish brown. The legs and bill are black throughout the year. Of similar size is the purple sandpiper, *Calidris maritima*, a dark, plump wader with yellowish legs, found mainly in winter on rocky shores.

### 'Tube-noses'

The 'tube-noses' are oceanic birds, mostly feeding on plankton, and coming to land only to nest. The group includes the petrels, fulmars, shearwaters and, in the southern hemisphere, the albatrosses. They have tubular nostrils, and a bill which curves down at the tip and is often hooked.

The storm petrel, *Hydrobates pelagicus* (Plate **63**, *6*), breeds on a number of rocky islands off our coasts, nesting in holes and burrows. It is small, only six inches long, and because of its blackish plumage and contrasting white rump it has been likened to a marine house martin. It flutters low over the water, often in the wake of ships, unlike its slightly larger relative, Leach's petrel, *Oceanodroma leucorhoa*, which does not follow ships habitually. The two petrels are hard to distinguish from each other, but Leach's petrel has a forked tail, whereas that of the storm petrel is squared.

Shearwaters are larger, the Manx shearwater, *Procellaria puffinus* (Plate **63**, *7*), being the species most often encountered off British coasts. A long-winged bird, it glides over the sea, banking steeply first one way and then the other, so that it shows its blackish upper parts and white underparts alternately.

The fulmar, *Fulmarus glacialis* (Plate **63**, *8*), also exhibits great mastery of the air. About eighteen inches long, grey above and white below, it might be mistaken for a plump gull, but can be distinguished by its 'tube-nose' bill and its method of gliding on straight, stiffly held wings, sometimes banking steeply like a shearwater. It now breeds on most British cliffs, having spread remarkably during the past century.

**Plate 64**  DUCKS AND DIVERS

1. Scaup, *Aythya marila* : 19 in.  2. Long-tailed duck, *Clangula hyemalis* : 21 in.  3. Common scoter, *Melanitta nigra* : 19 in. 4. Eider, *Somateria mollissima* : 23 in.  5. Red-breasted merganser, *Mergus serrator* : 23 in.  6. Shelduck, *Tadorna tadorna* : 24 in.  7. Red-throated diver, *Gavia stellata* : 24 in.  8. Slavonian grebe, *Podiceps auritus* (winter) : 13 in.

## Geese and ducks

Many species of ducks and geese frequent the coast, especially in winter. Four of those illustrated habitually dive for their food—molluscs, crustaceans and other invertebrates. The scaup, *Aythya marila*, and the long-tailed duck, *Clangula hyemalis* (Plate **64**, *1*, *2*), are visitors from breeding-grounds in northern Europe, as are most of the common scoters, *Melanitta nigra* (Plate **64**, *3*). The goldeneye, *Bucephala clangula*, and the velvet scoter, *Melanitta fusca*, are also migrant ducks that winter off our coasts.

The eider, *Somateria mollissima* (Plate **64**, *4*), however, is resident, nesting on the Northumberland, Lancashire and Scottish coasts. It is a large duck with a curiously shaped head, the upper surface of the bill forming almost a straight line with the forehead. Were it not for this characteristic head profile the female might bear a superficial resemblance to a large, heavily built dark female mallard. The eider drake, however, is a fine bird in winter and spring, black and white with a pinkish breast and a touch of green on the back of the head. All ducks use the down from their breasts to line their nests, but none does so in such quantity as the eider—eiderdown is, in fact, ' farmed ' commercially in Scandinavia.

The red-breasted merganser, *Mergus serrator* (Plate **64**, *5*), also dives for its food, but belongs to a group of ducks known as ' sawbills '. It is a fish-eater, and its slender bill has a saw-like edge, enabling it to grip its slippery prey. Mergansers frequent sea-lochs and other sheltered inlets, and estuaries in winter.

Several surface-feeding ducks, notably the wigeon, *Anas penelope*, pintail, *Anas acuta*, and mallard, *Anas platyrhynchos*, as well as swans and certain geese, come to the shore in winter, especially to the salt-marshes and mud-flats. They are chiefly vegetable eaters and are attracted by the eel-grass and other plants as well as by the small invertebrates.

The shelduck, *Tadorna tadorna* (Plate **64**, *6*), in some ways intermediate between ducks and geese, is common on the sand and mud-flats near which it breeds. It is a black and white bird, about two feet long, with a dark green head and neck (looking black at a distance), a chestnut band round the breast and a red bill. Duck and drake have similar plumage but the duck is smaller. Shelduck feed on molluscs and other invertebrates obtainable at low tide.

Three species of diver winter on our coast. They can be distinguished from ducks by their dagger-like bills and their habit of swimming very low in the water. Their food consists of fish and the larger invertebrates. The red-throated diver, *Gavia stellata* (Plate **64**, *7*), is the species most often seen, but it lives up to its name only in its summer plumage. In winter its upper parts are greyish, finely marked with white spots, and its underparts white. The best distinguishing feature is, however, the bill, which appears uptilted. Grebes somewhat resemble divers, but are smaller and have shorter bodies. Among those wintering on our coasts is the Slavonian grebe, *Podiceps auritus* (Plate **64**, *8*).

## Rock pipits

Many small passerine (perching) birds are found on the coast, and one habitually lives there : the rock pipit, *Anthus spinoletta*, a dark olive-brown bird with a streaky breast. It is somewhat larger than the meadow pipit, with darker plumage and with grey, not white, outer tail feathers. It nests in holes or crannies in the cliffs and rocks, or in maritime vegetation, nearly always close to the shore.

## VERTEBRATES : MAMMALS

Mammals are warm-blooded vertebrates which produce live young (with a few exceptions in Australasia) and feed them on milk. Almost all of them are covered with fur, and most of them are land animals.

Some British land mammals will hunt or scavenge on the shore. Foxes, *Vulpes vulpes*, for example, will search for crabs on the rocks and will prey on nesting terns and black-headed gulls. The otter, *Lutra lutra*, will frequent estuaries and rocky shores, feeding on fish and crustaceans and often living in sea caves ; otters in western Scotland and the Hebrides live an almost entirely marine existence. Rats, usually common (or 'brown') rats, *Rattus norvegicus*, scavenge along the tide line after dark, and, besides eating refuse and any dead creatures which have been washed up, will consume crustaceans, molluscs and the eggs and young of sea-birds.

Seals and whales are specially equipped for marine life. They are all more or less streamlined in shape, and have a thick layer of fat (blubber) under their skins to help them to keep their body heat in the cold water. Although, like all mammals, they are air-breathing, they are specially adapted for staying under water for long periods.

The seals found around our coasts are very different from the performing seals seen at the circus, which are in fact sea-lions. True seals have their hind limbs pointing backwards and consequently they cannot be used to support the body on land. In the water, however, these hind feet are used to drive the animal along, while the short, fin-like fore limbs are held close to the sides. Thus when swimming the seal is shaped rather like a torpedo. Seals are inquisitive animals, and if disturbed from their 'hauling-out' places will watch the human intruder from the safety of the sea, with just their heads above water.

Two species breed in Britain : the common seal, *Phoca vitulina*, which usually measures less than six feet, and the grey seal, *Halichoerus grypus*, which often exceeds eight feet in length. The two are often hard to distinguish when in the water, especially if seen full face. Viewed sideways, however, the common seal is recognizable by its more rounded head and short muzzle ; the grey has a long head, especially the adult bull, which has a pronounced Roman nose. Colour is of little help for they are both very variable.

Common seals frequent sandbanks and estuaries and in England are most numerous on eastern shores, especially in the Wash. In Scotland they are commonest on the west side and around Orkney and Shetland. Grey seals prefer rocky coasts and are mainly found on the Atlantic coasts of Britain, breeding in Cornwall, Pembroke-shire and some of the Scottish islands. There is also an important colony on the Farnes, off Northumberland.

Seals still have to come ashore to breed, but whales are completely adapted for spending all their lives in the sea—so completely that at one time people thought they were fish. Most of them are fish-shaped and even have dorsal fins, but while a fish's tail is usually held vertically, the tail flukes of a whale are held horizontally. Whales evolved from land mammals. They have lost their hind limbs and their fore limbs have become flippers.

Some whales have teeth, while others have horny plates of ' whalebone ' or baleen through which they strain the plankton on which they feed. Both toothed and baleen whales occur round British coasts, and sick or dying animals are sometimes stranded on beaches. The porpoise, *Phocæna phocæna*, a toothed whale about four to six feet long, is the commonest species seen. It has a blunt head and is black above, greyish white below.

# STRANDED OBJECTS

Several rather cryptic-looking objects are sometimes cast up on the seashore. Flattish white
' bones ' are the internal shells of cuttlefish
(Plate **49**, *1a*) ; and tapering greyish cylinders,
resembling large slate pencils, are those of the
belemnites, extinct creatures related to the cuttlefish. Wood bored with holes may have been
tunnelled by the so-called ship-worms (they are
really molluscs), *Teredo* (*see* p. 184), or by the
gribble (*see* p. 195). The ' mermaids' purses ',
objects a few inches long, pointed at their corners
(Plate **44**, *10*), are the empty egg cases of such
coastal fish as dogfish, skates or rays. A rounded
lump of sand-coloured material, also a few inches
long, consists of the empty egg capsules of the
whelk.

# INDEX

247

248

249

*Printed in England
by Taylowe Ltd.
Maidenhead*